Disability Discrimination Act 1995

CHAPTER 50

ARRANGEMENT OF SECTIONS

Disability Discrimination Act 1995

1995 CHAPTER 50

An Act to make it unlawful to discriminate against disabled persons in connection with employment, the provision of goods, facilities and services or the disposal or management of premises; to make provision about the employment of disabled persons; and to establish a National Disability Council. [8th November 1995]

BE IT ENACTED by the Queen's most Excellent Majesty, by and with the advice and consent of the Lords Spiritual and Temporal, and Commons, in this present Parliament assembled, and by the authority of the same, as follows:—

PART I

DISABILITY

1.—(1) Subject to the provisions of Schedule 1, a person has a disability for the purposes of this Act if he has a physical or mental impairment which has a substantial and long-term adverse effect on his ability to carry out normal day-to-day activities.

Meaning of "disability" and "disabled person".

(2) In this Act "disabled person" means a person who has a disability.

2.—(1) The provisions of this Part and Parts II and III apply in relation to a person who has had a disability as they apply in relation to a person who has that disability.

Past disabilities.

(2) Those provisions are subject to the modifications made by Schedule 2.

(3) Any regulations or order made under this Act may include provision with respect to persons who have had a disability.

(4) In any proceedings under Part II or Part III of this Act, the question whether a person had a disability at a particular time ("the relevant time") shall be determined, for the purposes of this section, as if the provisions of, or made under, this Act in force when the act complained of was done had been in force at the relevant time.

PART I

(5) The relevant time may be a time before the passing of this Act.

Guidance.

3.—(1) The Secretary of State may issue guidance about the matters to be taken into account in determining—

   (a) whether an impairment has a substantial adverse effect on a person's ability to carry out normal day-to-day activities; or

   (b) whether such an impairment has a long-term effect.

(2) The guidance may, among other things, give examples of—

   (a) effects which it would be reasonable, in relation to particular activities, to regard for purposes of this Act as substantial adverse effects;

   (b) effects which it would not be reasonable, in relation to particular activities, to regard for such purposes as substantial adverse effects;

   (c) substantial adverse effects which it would be reasonable to regard, for such purposes, as long-term;

   (d) substantial adverse effects which it would not be reasonable to regard, for such purposes, as long-term.

(3) A tribunal or court determining, for any purpose of this Act, whether an impairment has a substantial and long-term adverse effect on a person's ability to carry out normal day-to-day activities, shall take into account any guidance which appears to it to be relevant.

(4) In preparing a draft of any guidance, the Secretary of State shall consult such persons as he considers appropriate.

(5) Where the Secretary of State proposes to issue any guidance, he shall publish a draft of it, consider any representations that are made to him about the draft and, if he thinks it appropriate, modify his proposals in the light of any of those representations.

(6) If the Secretary of State decides to proceed with any proposed guidance, he shall lay a draft of it before each House of Parliament.

(7) If, within the 40-day period, either House resolves not to approve the draft, the Secretary of State shall take no further steps in relation to the proposed guidance.

(8) If no such resolution is made within the 40-day period, the Secretary of State shall issue the guidance in the form of his draft.

(9) The guidance shall come into force on such date as the Secretary of State may appoint by order.

(10) Subsection (7) does not prevent a new draft of the proposed guidance from being laid before Parliament.

(11) The Secretary of State may—

   (a) from time to time revise the whole or part of any guidance and re-issue it;

   (b) by order revoke any guidance.

(12) In this section—

   "40-day period", in relation to the draft of any proposed guidance, means—

(a) if the draft is laid before one House on a day later than the day on which it is laid before the other House, the period of 40 days beginning with the later of the two days, and

(b) in any other case, the period of 40 days beginning with the day on which the draft is laid before each House,

no account being taken of any period during which Parliament is dissolved or prorogued or during which both Houses are adjourned for more than 4 days; and

"guidance" means guidance issued by the Secretary of State under this section and includes guidance which has been revised and re-issued.

PART II

EMPLOYMENT

Discrimination by employers

4.—(1) It is unlawful for an employer to discriminate against a disabled person—

(a) in the arrangements which he makes for the purpose of determining to whom he should offer employment;

(b) in the terms on which he offers that person employment; or

(c) by refusing to offer, or deliberately not offering, him employment.

(2) It is unlawful for an employer to discriminate against a disabled person whom he employs—

(a) in the terms of employment which he affords him;

(b) in the opportunities which he affords him for promotion, a transfer, training or receiving any other benefit;

(c) by refusing to afford him, or deliberately not affording him, any such opportunity; or

(d) by dismissing him, or subjecting him to any other detriment.

(3) Subsection (2) does not apply to benefits of any description if the employer is concerned with the provision (whether or not for payment) of benefits of that description to the public, or to a section of the public which includes the employee in question, unless—

(a) that provision differs in a material respect from the provision of the benefits by the employer to his employees; or

(b) the provision of the benefits to the employee in question is regulated by his contract of employment; or

(c) the benefits relate to training.

(4) In this Part "benefits" includes facilities and services.

(5) In the case of an act which constitutes discrimination by virtue of section 55, this section also applies to discrimination against a person who is not disabled.

(6) This section applies only in relation to employment at an establishment in Great Britain.

Discrimination against applicants and employees.

5.—(1) For the purposes of this Part, an employer discriminates against a disabled person if—

    (a) for a reason which relates to the disabled person's disability, he treats him less favourably than he treats or would treat others to whom that reason does not or would not apply; and

    (b) he cannot show that the treatment in question is justified.

(2) For the purposes of this Part, an employer also discriminates against a disabled person if—

    (a) he fails to comply with a section 6 duty imposed on him in relation to the disabled person; and

    (b) he cannot show that his failure to comply with that duty is justified.

(3) Subject to subsection (5), for the purposes of subsection (1) treatment is justified if, but only if, the reason for it is both material to the circumstances of the particular case and substantial.

(4) For the purposes of subsection (2), failure to comply with a section 6 duty is justified if, but only if, the reason for the failure is both material to the circumstances of the particular case and substantial.

(5) If, in a case falling within subsection (1), the employer is under a section 6 duty in relation to the disabled person but fails without justification to comply with that duty, his treatment of that person cannot be justified under subsection (3) unless it would have been justified even if he had complied with the section 6 duty.

(6) Regulations may make provision, for purposes of this section, as to circumstances in which—

    (a) treatment is to be taken to be justified;

    (b) failure to comply with a section 6 duty is to be taken to be justified;

    (c) treatment is to be taken not to be justified;

    (d) failure to comply with a section 6 duty is to be taken not to be justified.

(7) Regulations under subsection (6) may, in particular—

    (a) make provision by reference to the cost of affording any benefit; and

    (b) in relation to benefits under occupational pension schemes, make provision with a view to enabling uniform rates of contributions to be maintained.

6.—(1) Where—

    (a) any arrangements made by or on behalf of an employer, or

    (b) any physical feature of premises occupied by the employer,

place the disabled person concerned at a substantial disadvantage in comparison with persons who are not disabled, it is the duty of the employer to take such steps as it is reasonable, in all the circumstances of the case, for him to have to take in order to prevent the arrangements or feature having that effect.

(2) Subsection (1)(a) applies only in relation to—

(a) arrangements for determining to whom employment should be offered;

(b) any term, condition or arrangements on which employment, promotion, a transfer, training or any other benefit is offered or afforded.

(3) The following are examples of steps which an employer may have to take in relation to a disabled person in order to comply with subsection (1)—

(a) making adjustments to premises;

(b) allocating some of the disabled person's duties to another person;

(c) transferring him to fill an existing vacancy;

(d) altering his working hours;

(e) assigning him to a different place of work;

(f) allowing him to be absent during working hours for rehabilitation, assessment or treatment;

(g) giving him, or arranging for him to be given, training;

(h) acquiring or modifying equipment;

(i) modifying instructions or reference manuals;

(j) modifying procedures for testing or assessment;

(k) providing a reader or interpreter;

(l) providing supervision.

(4) In determining whether it is reasonable for an employer to have to take a particular step in order to comply with subsection (1), regard shall be had, in particular, to—

(a) the extent to which taking the step would prevent the effect in question;

(b) the extent to which it is practicable for the employer to take the step;

(c) the financial and other costs which would be incurred by the employer in taking the step and the extent to which taking it would disrupt any of his activities;

(d) the extent of the employer's financial and other resources;

(e) the availability to the employer of financial or other assistance with respect to taking the step.

This subsection is subject to any provision of regulations made under subsection (8).

(5) In this section, "the disabled person concerned" means—

(a) in the case of arrangements for determining to whom employment should be offered, any disabled person who is, or has notified the employer that he may be, an applicant for that employment;

(b) in any other case, a disabled person who is—

(i) an applicant for the employment concerned; or

(ii) an employee of the employer concerned.

PART II

(6) Nothing in this section imposes any duty on an employer in relation to a disabled person if the employer does not know, and could not reasonably be expected to know—

> (a) in the case of an applicant or potential applicant, that the disabled person concerned is, or may be, an applicant for the employment; or
>
> (b) in any case, that that person has a disability and is likely to be affected in the way mentioned in subsection (1).

(7) Subject to the provisions of this section, nothing in this Part is to be taken to require an employer to treat a disabled person more favourably than he treats or would treat others.

(8) Regulations may make provision, for the purposes of subsection (1)—

> (a) as to circumstances in which arrangements are, or a physical feature is, to be taken to have the effect mentioned in that subsection;
>
> (b) as to circumstances in which arrangements are not, or a physical feature is not, to be taken to have that effect;
>
> (c) as to circumstances in which it is reasonable for an employer to have to take steps of a prescribed description;
>
> (d) as to steps which it is always reasonable for an employer to have to take;
>
> (e) as to circumstances in which it is not reasonable for an employer to have to take steps of a prescribed description;
>
> (f) as to steps which it is never reasonable for an employer to have to take;
>
> (g) as to things which are to be treated as physical features;
>
> (h) as to things which are not to be treated as such features.

(9) Regulations made under subsection (8)(c), (d), (e) or (f) may, in particular, make provision by reference to the cost of taking the steps concerned.

(10) Regulations may make provision adding to the duty imposed on employers by this section, including provision of a kind which may be made under subsection (8).

(11) This section does not apply in relation to any benefit under an occupational pension scheme or any other benefit payable in money or money's worth under a scheme or arrangement for the benefit of employees in respect of—

> (a) termination of service;
>
> (b) retirement, old age or death;
>
> (c) accident, injury, sickness or invalidity; or
>
> (d) any other prescribed matter.

(12) This section imposes duties only for the purpose of determining whether an employer has discriminated against a disabled person; and accordingly a breach of any such duty is not actionable as such.

Exemption for small businesses.

7.—(1) Nothing in this Part applies in relation to an employer who has fewer than 20 employees.

(2) The Secretary of State may by order amend subsection (1) by substituting a different number (not greater than 20) for the number for the time being specified there.

(3) In this section—

"anniversary" means the anniversary of the coming into force of this section; and

"review" means a review of the effect of this section.

(4) Before making any order under subsection (2), the Secretary of State shall conduct a review.

(5) Unless he has already begun or completed a review under subsection (4), the Secretary of State shall begin to conduct a review immediately after the fourth anniversary.

(6) Any review shall be completed within nine months.

(7) In conducting any review, the Secretary of State shall consult—

(a) such organisations representing the interests of employers as he considers appropriate; and

(b) such organisations representing the interests of disabled persons in employment or seeking employment as he considers appropriate.

(8) If, on completing a review, the Secretary of State decides to make an order under subsection (2), he shall make such an order to come into force not later than one year after the commencement of the review.

(9) If, on completing a review, the Secretary of State decides not to make such an order, he shall not later than one year after the commencement of the review lay before Parliament a report—

(a) summarising the results of the review; and

(b) giving the reasons for his decision.

(10) Any report made by the Secretary of State under subsection (9) shall include a summary of the views expressed to him in his consultations.

Enforcement etc.

8.—(1) A complaint by any person that another person—

(a) has discriminated against him in a way which is unlawful under this Part, or

(b) is, by virtue of section 57 or 58, to be treated as having discriminated against him in such a way,

may be presented to an industrial tribunal.

Enforcement, remedies and procedure.

(2) Where an industrial tribunal finds that a complaint presented to it under this section is well-founded, it shall take such of the following steps as it considers just and equitable—

(a) making a declaration as to the rights of the complainant and the respondent in relation to the matters to which the complaint relates;

(b) ordering the respondent to pay compensation to the complainant;

(c) recommending that the respondent take, within a specified period, action appearing to the tribunal to be reasonable, in all the circumstances of the case, for the purpose of obviating or reducing the adverse effect on the complainant of any matter to which the complaint relates.

(3) Where a tribunal orders compensation under subsection (2)(b), the amount of the compensation shall be calculated by applying the principles applicable to the calculation of damages in claims in tort or (in Scotland) in reparation for breach of statutory duty.

(4) For the avoidance of doubt it is hereby declared that compensation in respect of discrimination in a way which is unlawful under this Part may include compensation for injury to feelings whether or not it includes compensation under any other head.

(5) If the respondent to a complaint fails, without reasonable justification, to comply with a recommendation made by an industrial tribunal under subsection (2)(c) the tribunal may, if it thinks it just and equitable to do so—

(a) increase the amount of compensation required to be paid to the complainant in respect of the complaint, where an order was made under subsection (2)(b); or

(b) make an order under subsection (2)(b).

(6) Regulations may make provision—

(a) for enabling a tribunal, where an amount of compensation falls to be awarded under subsection (2)(b), to include in the award interest on that amount; and

(b) specifying, for cases where a tribunal decides that an award is to include an amount in respect of interest, the manner in which and the periods and rate by reference to which the interest is to be determined.

1978 c. 44.

(7) Regulations may modify the operation of any order made under paragraph 6A of Schedule 9 to the Employment Protection (Consolidation) Act 1978 (power to make provision as to interest on sums payable in pursuance of industrial tribunal decisions) to the extent that it relates to an award of compensation under subsection (2)(b).

(8) Part I of Schedule 3 makes further provision about the enforcement of this Part and about procedure.

Validity of certain agreements.

9.—(1) Any term in a contract of employment or other agreement is void so far as it purports to—

(a) require a person to do anything which would contravene any provision of, or made under, this Part;

(b) exclude or limit the operation of any provision of this Part; or

(c) prevent any person from presenting a complaint to an industrial tribunal under this Part.

(2) Paragraphs (b) and (c) of subsection (1) do not apply to an agreement not to institute proceedings under section 8(1), or to an agreement not to continue such proceedings, if—

(a) a conciliation officer has acted under paragraph 1 of Schedule 3 in relation to the matter; or

(b) the conditions set out in subsection (3) are satisfied.

(3) The conditions are that—

(a) the complainant must have received independent legal advice from a qualified lawyer as to the terms and effect of the proposed agreement (and in particular its effect on his ability to pursue his complaint before an industrial tribunal);

(b) when the adviser gave the advice there must have been in force a policy of insurance covering the risk of a claim by the complainant in respect of loss arising in consequence of the advice; and

(c) the agreement must be in writing, relate to the particular complaint, identify the adviser and state that the conditions are satisfied.

(4) In this section—

"independent", in relation to legal advice to the complainant, means that it is given by a lawyer who is not acting for the other party or for a person who is connected with that other party; and

"qualified lawyer" means—

(a) as respects proceedings in England and Wales, a barrister (whether in practice as such or employed to give legal advice) or a solicitor of the Supreme Court who holds a practising certificate; and

(b) as respects proceedings in Scotland, an advocate (whether in practice as such or employed to give legal advice) or a solicitor who holds a practising certificate.

(5) For the purposes of subsection (4), any two persons are to be treated as connected if—

(a) one is a company of which the other (directly or indirectly) has control, or

(b) both are companies of which a third person (directly or indirectly) has control.

10.—(1) Nothing in this Part—

(a) affects any charitable instrument which provides for conferring benefits on one or more categories of person determined by reference to any physical or mental capacity; or

(b) makes unlawful any act done by a charity or recognised body in pursuance of any of its charitable purposes, so far as those purposes are connected with persons so determined.

Charities and support for particular groups of persons.

(2) Nothing in this Part prevents—

(a) a person who provides supported employment from treating members of a particular group of disabled persons more favourably than other persons in providing such employment; or

(b) the Secretary of State from agreeing to arrangements for the provision of supported employment which will, or may, have that effect.

(3) In this section—

"charitable instrument" means an enactment or other instrument (whenever taking effect) so far as it relates to charitable purposes;

1993 c. 10.
"charity" has the same meaning as in the Charities Act 1993;

1990 c. 40.
"recognised body" means a body which is a recognised body for the purposes of Part I of the Law Reform (Miscellaneous Provisions) (Scotland) Act 1990; and

1944 c. 10.
"supported employment" means facilities provided, or in respect of which payments are made, under section 15 of the Disabled Persons (Employment) Act 1944.

(4) In the application of this section to England and Wales, "charitable purposes" means purposes which are exclusively charitable according to the law of England and Wales.

(5) In the application of this section to Scotland, "charitable purposes" shall be construed in the same way as if it were contained in the Income Tax Acts.

Advertisements suggesting that employers will discriminate against disabled persons.

11.—(1) This section applies where—

(a) a disabled person has applied for employment with an employer;

(b) the employer has refused to offer, or has deliberately not offered, him the employment;

(c) the disabled person has presented a complaint under section 8 against the employer;

(d) the employer has advertised the employment (whether before or after the disabled person applied for it); and

(e) the advertisement indicated, or might reasonably be understood to have indicated, that any application for the advertised employment would, or might, be determined to any extent by reference to—

　　(i) the successful applicant not having any disability or any category of disability which includes the disabled person's disability; or

　　(ii) the employer's reluctance to take any action of a kind mentioned in section 6.

(2) The tribunal hearing the complaint shall assume, unless the contrary is shown, that the employer's reason for refusing to offer, or deliberately not offering, the employment to the complainant was related to the complainant's disability.

(3) In this section "advertisement" includes every form of advertisement or notice, whether to the public or not.

Discrimination by other persons

Discrimination against contract workers.

12.—(1) It is unlawful for a principal, in relation to contract work, to discriminate against a disabled person—

(a) in the terms on which he allows him to do that work;

(b) by not allowing him to do it or continue to do it;

(c) in the way he affords him access to any benefits or by refusing or deliberately omitting to afford him access to them; or

(d) by subjecting him to any other detriment.

(2) Subsection (1) does not apply to benefits of any description if the principal is concerned with the provision (whether or not for payment) of benefits of that description to the public, or to a section of the public which includes the contract worker in question, unless that provision differs in a material respect from the provision of the benefits by the principal to contract workers.

(3) The provisions of this Part (other than subsections (1) to (3) of section 4) apply to any principal, in relation to contract work, as if he were, or would be, the employer of the contract worker and as if any contract worker supplied to do work for him were an employee of his.

(4) In the case of an act which constitutes discrimination by virtue of section 55, this section also applies to discrimination against a person who is not disabled.

(5) This section applies only in relation to contract work done at an establishment in Great Britain (the provisions of section 68 about the meaning of "employment at an establishment in Great Britain" applying for the purposes of this subsection with the appropriate modifications).

(6) In this section—

"principal" means a person ("A") who makes work available for doing by individuals who are employed by another person who supplies them under a contract made with A;

"contract work" means work so made available; and

"contract worker" means any individual who is supplied to the principal under such a contract.

13.—(1) It is unlawful for a trade organisation to discriminate against a disabled person—

    (a) in the terms on which it is prepared to admit him to membership of the organisation; or

    (b) by refusing to accept, or deliberately not accepting, his application for membership.

Discrimination by trade organisations.

(2) It is unlawful for a trade organisation, in the case of a disabled person who is a member of the organisation, to discriminate against him—

    (a) in the way it affords him access to any benefits or by refusing or deliberately omitting to afford him access to them;

    (b) by depriving him of membership, or varying the terms on which he is a member; or

    (c) by subjecting him to any other detriment.

(3) In the case of an act which constitutes discrimination by virtue of section 55, this section also applies to discrimination against a person who is not disabled.

(4) In this section "trade organisation" means an organisation of workers, an organisation of employers or any other organisation whose members carry on a particular profession or trade for the purposes of which the organisation exists.

14.—(1) For the purposes of this Part, a trade organisation discriminates against a disabled person if—

Meaning of "discrimination" in relation to trade organisations.

(a) for a reason which relates to the disabled person's disability, it treats him less favourably than it treats or would treat others to whom that reason does not or would not apply; and

(b) it cannot show that the treatment in question is justified.

(2) For the purposes of this Part, a trade organisation also discriminates against a disabled person if—

(a) it fails to comply with a section 15 duty imposed on it in relation to the disabled person; and

(b) it cannot show that its failure to comply with that duty is justified.

(3) Subject to subsection (5), for the purposes of subsection (1) treatment is justified if, but only if, the reason for it is both material to the circumstances of the particular case and substantial.

(4) For the purposes of subsection (2), failure to comply with a section 15 duty is justified if, but only if, the reason for the failure is both material to the circumstances of the particular case and substantial.

(5) If, in a case falling within subsection (1), the trade organisation is under a section 15 duty in relation to the disabled person concerned but fails without justification to comply with that duty, its treatment of that person cannot be justified under subsection (3) unless the treatment would have been justified even if the organisation had complied with the section 15 duty.

(6) Regulations may make provision, for purposes of this section, as to circumstances in which—

(a) treatment is to be taken to be justified;

(b) failure to comply with a section 15 duty is to be taken to be justified;

(c) treatment is to be taken not to be justified;

(d) failure to comply with a section 15 duty is to be taken not to be justified.

Duty of trade organisation to make adjustments.

15.—(1) Where—

(a) any arrangements made by or on behalf of a trade organisation, or

(b) any physical feature of premises occupied by the organisation,

place the disabled person concerned at a substantial disadvantage in comparison with persons who are not disabled, it is the duty of the organisation to take such steps as it is reasonable, in all the circumstances of the case, for it to have to take in order to prevent the arrangements or feature having that effect.

(2) Subsection (1)(a) applies only in relation to—

(a) arrangements for determining who should become or remain a member of the organisation;

(b) any term, condition or arrangements on which membership or any benefit is offered or afforded.

(3) In determining whether it is reasonable for a trade organisation to have to take a particular step in order to comply with subsection (1), regard shall be had, in particular, to—

(a) the extent to which taking the step would prevent the effect in question;

(b) the extent to which it is practicable for the organisation to take the step;

(c) the financial and other costs which would be incurred by the organisation in taking the step and the extent to which taking it would disrupt any of its activities;

(d) the extent of the organisation's financial and other resources;

(e) the availability to the organisation of financial or other assistance with respect to taking the step.

This subsection is subject to any provision of regulations made under subsection (7).

(4) In this section "the disabled person concerned" means—

(a) in the case of arrangements for determining to whom membership should be offered, any disabled person who is, or has notified the organisation that he may be, an applicant for membership;

(b) in any other case, a disabled person who is—

(i) an applicant for membership; or

(ii) a member of the organisation.

(5) Nothing in this section imposes any duty on an organisation in relation to a disabled person if the organisation does not know, and could not reasonably be expected to know that the disabled person concerned—

(a) is, or may be, an applicant for membership; or

(b) has a disability and is likely to be affected in the way mentioned in subsection (1).

(6) Subject to the provisions of this section, nothing in this Part is to be taken to require a trade organisation to treat a disabled person more favourably than it treats or would treat others.

(7) Regulations may make provision for the purposes of subsection (1) as to any of the matters mentioned in paragraphs (a) to (h) of section 6(8) (the references in those paragraphs to an employer being read for these purposes as references to a trade organisation).

(8) Subsection (9) of section 6 applies in relation to such regulations as it applies in relation to regulations made under section 6(8).

(9) Regulations may make provision adding to the duty imposed on trade organisations by this section, including provision of a kind which may be made under subsection (7).

(10) This section imposes duties only for the purpose of determining whether a trade organisation has discriminated against a disabled person; and accordingly a breach of any such duty is not actionable as such.

Premises occupied under leases

16.—(1) This section applies where—

(a) an employer or trade organisation ("the occupier") occupies premises under a lease;

(b) but for this section, the occupier would not be entitled to make a particular alteration to the premises; and

(c) the alteration is one which the occupier proposes to make in order to comply with a section 6 duty or section 15 duty.

(2) Except to the extent to which it expressly so provides, the lease shall have effect by virtue of this subsection as if it provided—

(a) for the occupier to be entitled to make the alteration with the written consent of the lessor;

(b) for the occupier to have to make a written application to the lessor for consent if he wishes to make the alteration;

(c) if such an application is made, for the lessor not to withhold his consent unreasonably; and

(d) for the lessor to be entitled to make his consent subject to reasonable conditions.

(3) In this section—

"lease" includes a tenancy, sub-lease or sub-tenancy and an agreement for a lease, tenancy, sub-lease or sub-tenancy; and

"sub-lease" and "sub-tenancy" have such meaning as may be prescribed.

(4) If the terms and conditions of a lease—

(a) impose conditions which are to apply if the occupier alters the premises, or

(b) entitle the lessor to impose conditions when consenting to the occupier's altering the premises,

the occupier is to be treated for the purposes of subsection (1) as not being entitled to make the alteration.

(5) Part I of Schedule 4 supplements the provisions of this section.

Occupational pension schemes and insurance services

17.—(1) Every occupational pension scheme shall be taken to include a provision ("a non-discrimination rule")—

(a) relating to the terms on which—

(i) persons become members of the scheme; and

(ii) members of the scheme are treated; and

(b) requiring the trustees or managers of the scheme to refrain from any act or omission which, if done in relation to a person by an employer, would amount to unlawful discrimination against that person for the purposes of this Part.

(2) The other provisions of the scheme are to have effect subject to the non-discrimination rule.

(3) Without prejudice to section 67, regulations under this Part may—

(a) with respect to trustees or managers of occupational pension schemes make different provision from that made with respect to employers; or

(b) make provision modifying the application to such trustees or managers of any regulations made under this Part, or of any provisions of this Part so far as they apply to employers.

(4) In determining, for the purposes of this section, whether an act or omission would amount to unlawful discrimination if done by an employer, any provision made under subsection (3) shall be applied as if it applied in relation to the notional employer.

18.—(1) This section applies where a provider of insurance services ("the insurer") enters into arrangements with an employer under which the employer's employees, or a class of his employees—

Insurance services.

(a) receive insurance services provided by the insurer; or

(b) are given an opportunity to receive such services.

(2) The insurer is to be taken, for the purposes of this Part, to discriminate unlawfully against a disabled person who is a relevant employee if he acts in relation to that employee in a way which would be unlawful discrimination for the purposes of Part III if—

(a) he were providing the service in question to members of the public; and

(b) the employee was provided with, or was trying to secure the provision of, that service as a member of the public.

(3) In this section—

"insurance services" means services of a prescribed description for the provision of benefits in respect of—

(a) termination of service;

(b) retirement, old age or death;

(c) accident, injury, sickness or invalidity; or

(d) any other prescribed matter; and

"relevant employee" means—

(a) in the case of an arrangement which applies to employees of the employer in question, an employee of his;

(b) in the case of an arrangement which applies to a class of employees of the employer, an employee who is in that class.

(4) For the purposes of the definition of "relevant employee" in subsection (3), "employee", in relation to an employer, includes a person who has applied for, or is contemplating applying for, employment by that employer or (as the case may be) employment by him in the class in question.

Part III

Discrimination in Other Areas

Goods, facilities and services

Discrimination in relation to goods, facilities and services.

19.—(1) It is unlawful for a provider of services to discriminate against a disabled person—

(a) in refusing to provide, or deliberately not providing, to the disabled person any service which he provides, or is prepared to provide, to members of the public;

(b) in failing to comply with any duty imposed on him by section 21 in circumstances in which the effect of that failure is to make it impossible or unreasonably difficult for the disabled person to make use of any such service;

(c) in the standard of service which he provides to the disabled person or the manner in which he provides it to him; or

(d) in the terms on which he provides a service to the disabled person.

(2) For the purposes of this section and sections 20 and 21—

(a) the provision of services includes the provision of any goods or facilities;

(b) a person is "a provider of services" if he is concerned with the provision, in the United Kingdom, of services to the public or to a section of the public; and

(c) it is irrelevant whether a service is provided on payment or without payment.

(3) The following are examples of services to which this section and sections 20 and 21 apply—

(a) access to and use of any place which members of the public are permitted to enter;

(b) access to and use of means of communication;

(c) access to and use of information services;

(d) accommodation in a hotel, boarding house or other similar establishment;

(e) facilities by way of banking or insurance or for grants, loans, credit or finance;

(f) facilities for entertainment, recreation or refreshment;

1973 c. 50.

(g) facilities provided by employment agencies or under section 2 of the Employment and Training Act 1973;

(h) the services of any profession or trade, or any local or other public authority.

(4) In the case of an act which constitutes discrimination by virtue of section 55, this section also applies to discrimination against a person who is not disabled.

(5) Except in such circumstances as may be prescribed, this section and sections 20 and 21 do not apply to—

  (a) education which is funded, or secured, by a relevant body or provided at—

      (i) an establishment which is funded by such a body or by a Minister of the Crown; or

      (ii) any other establishment which is a school as defined in section 14(5) of the Further and Higher Education Act 1992 or section 135(1) of the Education (Scotland) Act 1980;

  (b) any service so far as it consists of the use of any means of transport; or

  (c) such other services as may be prescribed.

(in margin: 1992 c. 13. 1980 c. 44.)

(6) In subsection (5) "relevant body" means—

  (a) a local education authority in England and Wales;

  (b) an education authority in Scotland;

  (c) the Funding Agency for Schools;

  (d) the Schools Funding Council for Wales;

  (e) the Further Education Funding Council for England;

  (f) the Further Education Funding Council for Wales;

  (g) the Higher Education Funding Council for England;

  (h) the Scottish Higher Education Funding Council;

  (i) the Higher Education Funding Council for Wales;

  (j) the Teacher Training Agency;

  (k) a voluntary organisation; or

  (l) a body of a prescribed kind.

20.—(1) For the purposes of section 19, a provider of services discriminates against a disabled person if—

  (a) for a reason which relates to the disabled person's disability, he treats him less favourably than he treats or would treat others to whom that reason does not or would not apply; and

  (b) he cannot show that the treatment in question is justified.

(in margin: Meaning of "discrimination".)

(2) For the purposes of section 19, a provider of services also discriminates against a disabled person if—

  (a) he fails to comply with a section 21 duty imposed on him in relation to the disabled person; and

  (b) he cannot show that his failure to comply with that duty is justified.

(3) For the purposes of this section, treatment is justified only if—

  (a) in the opinion of the provider of services, one or more of the conditions mentioned in subsection (4) are satisfied; and

  (b) it is reasonable, in all the circumstances of the case, for him to hold that opinion.

(4) The conditions are that—

(a) in any case, the treatment is necessary in order not to endanger the health or safety of any person (which may include that of the disabled person);

(b) in any case, the disabled person is incapable of entering into an enforceable agreement, or of giving an informed consent, and for that reason the treatment is reasonable in that case;

(c) in a case falling within section 19(1)(a), the treatment is necessary because the provider of services would otherwise be unable to provide the service to members of the public;

(d) in a case falling within section 19(1)(c) or (d), the treatment is necessary in order for the provider of services to be able to provide the service to the disabled person or to other members of the public;

(e) in a case falling within section 19(1)(d), the difference in the terms on which the service is provided to the disabled person and those on which it is provided to other members of the public reflects the greater cost to the provider of services in providing the service to the disabled person.

(5) Any increase in the cost of providing a service to a disabled person which results from compliance by a provider of services with a section 21 duty shall be disregarded for the purposes of subsection (4)(e).

(6) Regulations may make provision, for purposes of this section, as to circumstances in which—

(a) it is reasonable for a provider of services to hold the opinion mentioned in subsection (3)(a);

(b) it is not reasonable for a provider of services to hold that opinion.

(7) Regulations may make provision for subsection (4)(b) not to apply in prescribed circumstances where—

(a) a person is acting for a disabled person under a power of attorney;

1983 c. 20.

(b) functions conferred by or under Part VII of the Mental Health Act 1983 are exercisable in relation to a disabled person's property or affairs; or

(c) powers are exercisable in Scotland in relation to a disabled person's property or affairs in consequence of the appointment of a curator bonis, tutor or judicial factor.

(8) Regulations may make provision, for purposes of this section, as to circumstances (other than those mentioned in subsection (4)) in which treatment is to be taken to be justified.

(9) In subsections (3), (4) and (8) "treatment" includes failure to comply with a section 21 duty.

Duty of providers of services to make adjustments.

21.—(1) Where a provider of services has a practice, policy or procedure which makes it impossible or unreasonably difficult for disabled persons to make use of a service which he provides, or is prepared to provide, to other members of the public, it is his duty to take such steps as it is reasonable, in all the circumstances of the case, for him to have to take in order to change that practice, policy or procedure so that it no longer has that effect.

(2) Where a physical feature (for example, one arising from the design or construction of a building or the approach or access to premises) makes it impossible or unreasonably difficult for disabled persons to make use of such a service, it is the duty of the provider of that service to take such steps as it is reasonable, in all the circumstances of the case, for him to have to take in order to—

(a) remove the feature;

(b) alter it so that it no longer has that effect;

(c) provide a reasonable means of avoiding the feature; or

(d) provide a reasonable alternative method of making the service in question available to disabled persons.

(3) Regulations may prescribe—

(a) matters which are to be taken into account in determining whether any provision of a kind mentioned in subsection (2)(c) or (d) is reasonable; and

(b) categories of providers of services to whom subsection (2) does not apply.

(4) Where an auxiliary aid or service (for example, the provision of information on audio tape or of a sign language interpreter) would—

(a) enable disabled persons to make use of a service which a provider of services provides, or is prepared to provide, to members of the public, or

(b) facilitate the use by disabled persons of such a service,

it is the duty of the provider of that service to take such steps as it is reasonable, in all the circumstances of the case, for him to have to take in order to provide that auxiliary aid or service.

(5) Regulations may make provision, for the purposes of this section—

(a) as to circumstances in which it is reasonable for a provider of services to have to take steps of a prescribed description;

(b) as to circumstances in which it is not reasonable for a provider of services to have to take steps of a prescribed description;

(c) as to what is to be included within the meaning of "practice, policy or procedure";

(d) as to what is not to be included within the meaning of that expression;

(e) as to things which are to be treated as physical features;

(f) as to things which are not to be treated as such features;

(g) as to things which are to be treated as auxiliary aids or services;

(h) as to things which are not to be treated as auxiliary aids or services.

(6) Nothing in this section requires a provider of services to take any steps which would fundamentally alter the nature of the service in question or the nature of his trade, profession or business.

(7) Nothing in this section requires a provider of services to take any steps which would cause him to incur expenditure exceeding the prescribed maximum.

(8) Regulations under subsection (7) may provide for the prescribed maximum to be calculated by reference to—

(a) aggregate amounts of expenditure incurred in relation to different cases;

(b) prescribed periods;

(c) services of a prescribed description;

(d) premises of a prescribed description; or

(e) such other criteria as may be prescribed.

(9) Regulations may provide, for the purposes of subsection (7), for expenditure incurred by one provider of services to be treated as incurred by another.

(10) This section imposes duties only for the purpose of determining whether a provider of services has discriminated against a disabled person; and accordingly a breach of any such duty is not actionable as such.

Premises

Discrimination in relation to premises.

22.—(1) It is unlawful for a person with power to dispose of any premises to discriminate against a disabled person—

(a) in the terms on which he offers to dispose of those premises to the disabled person;

(b) by refusing to dispose of those premises to the disabled person; or

(c) in his treatment of the disabled person in relation to any list of persons in need of premises of that description.

(2) Subsection (1) does not apply to a person who owns an estate or interest in the premises and wholly occupies them unless, for the purpose of disposing of the premises, he—

(a) uses the services of an estate agent, or

(b) publishes an advertisement or causes an advertisement to be published.

(3) It is unlawful for a person managing any premises to discriminate against a disabled person occupying those premises—

(a) in the way he permits the disabled person to make use of any benefits or facilities;

(b) by refusing or deliberately omitting to permit the disabled person to make use of any benefits or facilities; or

(c) by evicting the disabled person, or subjecting him to any other detriment.

(4) It is unlawful for any person whose licence or consent is required for the disposal of any premises comprised in, or (in Scotland) the subject of, a tenancy to discriminate against a disabled person by withholding his licence or consent for the disposal of the premises to the disabled person.

(5) Subsection (4) applies to tenancies created before as well as after the passing of this Act.

(6) In this section—

"advertisement" includes every form of advertisement or notice, whether to the public or not;

"dispose", in relation to premises, includes granting a right to occupy the premises, and, in relation to premises comprised in, or (in Scotland) the subject of, a tenancy, includes—

    (a) assigning the tenancy, and

    (b) sub-letting or parting with possession of the premises or any part of the premises;

and "disposal" shall be construed accordingly;

"estate agent" means a person who, by way of profession or trade, provides services for the purpose of finding premises for persons seeking to acquire them or assisting in the disposal of premises; and

"tenancy" means a tenancy created—

    (a) by a lease or sub-lease,

    (b) by an agreement for a lease or sub-lease,

    (c) by a tenancy agreement, or

    (d) in pursuance of any enactment.

(7) In the case of an act which constitutes discrimination by virtue of section 55, this section also applies to discrimination against a person who is not disabled.

(8) This section applies only in relation to premises in the United Kingdom.

23.—(1) Where the conditions mentioned in subsection (2) are satisfied, subsection (1), (3) or (as the case may be) (4) of section 22 does not apply.   Exemption for small dwellings.

(2) The conditions are that—

    (a) the relevant occupier resides, and intends to continue to reside, on the premises;

    (b) the relevant occupier shares accommodation on the premises with persons who reside on the premises and are not members of his household;

    (c) the shared accommodation is not storage accommodation or a means of access; and

    (d) the premises are small premises.

(3) For the purposes of this section, premises are "small premises" if they fall within subsection (4) or (5).

(4) Premises fall within this subsection if—

    (a) only the relevant occupier and members of his household reside in the accommodation occupied by him;

    (b) the premises comprise, in addition to the accommodation occupied by the relevant occupier, residential accommodation for at least one other household;

    (c) the residential accommodation for each other household is let, or available for letting, on a separate tenancy or similar agreement; and

    (d) there are not normally more than two such other households.

(5) Premises fall within this subsection if there is not normally residential accommodation on the premises for more than six persons in addition to the relevant occupier and any members of his household.

(6) For the purposes of this section "the relevant occupier" means—

(a) in a case falling within section 22(1), the person with power to dispose of the premises, or a near relative of his;

(b) in a case falling within section 22(4), the person whose licence or consent is required for the disposal of the premises, or a near relative of his.

(7) For the purposes of this section—

"near relative" means a person's spouse, partner, parent, child, grandparent, grandchild, or brother or sister (whether of full or half blood or by affinity); and

"partner" means the other member of a couple consisting of a man and a woman who are not married to each other but are living together as husband and wife.

Meaning of "discrimination".

24.—(1) For the purposes of section 22, a person ("A") discriminates against a disabled person if—

(a) for a reason which relates to the disabled person's disability, he treats him less favourably than he treats or would treat others to whom that reason does not or would not apply; and

(b) he cannot show that the treatment in question is justified.

(2) For the purposes of this section, treatment is justified only if—

(a) in A's opinion, one or more of the conditions mentioned in subsection (3) are satisfied; and

(b) it is reasonable, in all the circumstances of the case, for him to hold that opinion.

(3) The conditions are that—

(a) in any case, the treatment is necessary in order not to endanger the health or safety of any person (which may include that of the disabled person);

(b) in any case, the disabled person is incapable of entering into an enforceable agreement, or of giving an informed consent, and for that reason the treatment is reasonable in that case;

(c) in a case falling within section 22(3)(a), the treatment is necessary in order for the disabled person or the occupiers of other premises forming part of the building to make use of the benefit or facility;

(d) in a case falling within section 22(3)(b), the treatment is necessary in order for the occupiers of other premises forming part of the building to make use of the benefit or facility.

(4) Regulations may make provision, for purposes of this section, as to circumstances in which—

(a) it is reasonable for a person to hold the opinion mentioned in subsection 2(a);

(b) it is not reasonable for a person to hold that opinion.

(5) Regulations may make provision, for purposes of this section, as to circumstances (other than those mentioned in subsection (3)) in which treatment is to be taken to be justified.

Enforcement, etc.

25.—(1) A claim by any person that another person—

   (a) has discriminated against him in a way which is unlawful under this Part; or

   (b) is by virtue of section 57 or 58 to be treated as having discriminated against him in such a way,

may be made the subject of civil proceedings in the same way as any other claim in tort or (in Scotland) in reparation for breach of statutory duty.

Enforcement, remedies and procedure.

(2) For the avoidance of doubt it is hereby declared that damages in respect of discrimination in a way which is unlawful under this Part may include compensation for injury to feelings whether or not they include compensation under any other head.

(3) Proceedings in England and Wales shall be brought only in a county court.

(4) Proceedings in Scotland shall be brought only in a sheriff court.

(5) The remedies available in such proceedings are those which are available in the High Court or (as the case may be) the Court of Session.

(6) Part II of Schedule 3 makes further provision about the enforcement of this Part and about procedure.

26.—(1) Any term in a contract for the provision of goods, facilities or services or in any other agreement is void so far as it purports to—

   (a) require a person to do anything which would contravene any provision of, or made under, this Part,

   (b) exclude or limit the operation of any provision of this Part, or

   (c) prevent any person from making a claim under this Part.

Validity and revision of certain agreements.

(2) Paragraphs (b) and (c) of subsection (1) do not apply to an agreement settling a claim to which section 25 applies.

(3) On the application of any person interested in an agreement to which subsection (1) applies, a county court or a sheriff court may make such order as it thinks just for modifying the agreement to take account of the effect of subsection (1).

(4) No such order shall be made unless all persons affected have been—

   (a) given notice of the application; and

   (b) afforded an opportunity to make representations to the court.

(5) Subsection (4) applies subject to any rules of court providing for that notice to be dispensed with.

(6) An order under subsection (3) may include provision as respects any period before the making of the order.

27.—(1) This section applies where—

   (a) a provider of services ("the occupier") occupies premises under a lease;

Alterations to premises occupied under leases.

(b) but for this section, he would not be entitled to make a particular alteration to the premises; and

(c) the alteration is one which the occupier proposes to make in order to comply with a section 21 duty.

(2) Except to the extent to which it expressly so provides, the lease shall have effect by virtue of this subsection as if it provided—

(a) for the occupier to be entitled to make the alteration with the written consent of the lessor;

(b) for the occupier to have to make a written application to the lessor for consent if he wishes to make the alteration;

(c) if such an application is made, for the lessor not to withhold his consent unreasonably; and

(d) for the lessor to be entitled to make his consent subject to reasonable conditions.

(3) In this section—

"lease" includes a tenancy, sub-lease or sub-tenancy and an agreement for a lease, tenancy, sub-lease or sub-tenancy; and

"sub-lease" and "sub-tenancy" have such meaning as may be prescribed.

(4) If the terms and conditions of a lease—

(a) impose conditions which are to apply if the occupier alters the premises, or

(b) entitle the lessor to impose conditions when consenting to the occupier's altering the premises,

the occupier is to be treated for the purposes of subsection (1) as not being entitled to make the alteration.

(5) Part II of Schedule 4 supplements the provisions of this section.

Advice and assistance.

28.—(1) The Secretary of State may make arrangements for the provision of advice and assistance to persons with a view to promoting the settlement of disputes arising under this Part otherwise than by recourse to the courts.

(2) Any person appointed by the Secretary of State in connection with arrangements made under subsection (1) shall have such duties as the Secretary of State may direct.

(3) The Secretary of State may pay to any person so appointed such allowances and compensation for loss of earnings as he considers appropriate.

(4) The Secretary of State may make such payments, by way of grants, in respect of expenditure incurred, or to be incurred, by any person exercising functions in accordance with arrangements made by the Secretary of State under this section as he considers appropriate.

(5) The approval of the Treasury is required for any payment under subsection (3) or (4).

PART IV

EDUCATION

29.—(1) In section 161(5) of the Education Act 1993 (information relating to pupils with special educational needs to be included in annual report), omit the words from "and in this subsection" to the end.

Education of disabled persons. 1993 c. 62.

(2) After section 161(5) of that Act insert—

"(6) The annual report for each county, voluntary or grant-maintained school shall include a report containing information as to—

(a) the arrangements for the admission of disabled pupils;

(b) the steps taken to prevent disabled pupils from being treated less favourably than other pupils; and

(c) the facilities provided to assist access to the school by disabled pupils.

(7) In this section—

"annual report" means the report prepared under the articles of government for the school in accordance with section 30 of the Education (No. 2) Act 1986 or, as the case may be, paragraph 8 of Schedule 6 to this Act; and

1986 c. 61.

"disabled pupils" means pupils who are disabled persons for the purposes of the Disability Discrimination Act 1995."

1995 c. 50.

(3) In section 1 of the Education Act 1994 (establishment of the Teacher Training Agency) add, at the end—

1994 c. 30.

"(4) In exercising their functions, the Teacher Training Agency shall have regard to the requirements of persons who are disabled persons for the purposes of the Disability Discrimination Act 1995."

30.—(1) The Further and Higher Education Act 1992 is amended as set out in subsections (2) to (6).

Further and higher education of disabled persons. 1992 c.13.

(2) In section 5 (administration of funds by further education funding councils), in subsection (6)(b), after "may" insert ", subject to subsection (7A) below,".

(3) After section 5(7) insert—

"(7A) Without prejudice to the power to impose conditions given by subsection (6)(b) above, the conditions subject to which a council gives financial support under this section to the governing body of an institution within the further education sector—

(a) shall require the governing body to publish disability statements at such intervals as may be prescribed; and

(b) may include conditions relating to the provision made, or to be made, by the institution with respect to disabled persons.

(7B) For the purposes of subsection (7A) above—

"disability statement" means a statement containing information of a prescribed description about the provision of facilities for education made by the institution in respect of disabled persons;

"disabled persons" means persons who are disabled persons for the purposes of the Disability Discrimination Act 1995; and

"prescribed" means prescribed by regulations."

(4) In section 8 (supplementary functions) add, at the end—

"(6) As soon as is reasonably practicable after the end of its financial year, each council shall make a written report to the Secretary of State on—

(a) the progress made during the year to which the report relates in the provision of further education for disabled students in their area; and

(b) their plans for the future provision of further education for disabled students in their area.

(7) In subsection (6) above—

"disabled students" means students who are disabled persons for the purposes of the Disability Discrimination Act 1995; and

"financial year" means the period of twelve months ending with 31st March 1997 and each successive period of twelve months."

(5) In section 62 (establishment of higher education funding councils), after subsection (7) insert—

"(7A) In exercising their functions, each council shall have regard to the requirements of disabled persons.

(7B) In subsection (7A) "disabled persons" means persons who are disabled persons for the purposes of the Disability Discrimination Act 1995."

(6) In section 65 (administration of funds by higher education funding councils), after subsection (4) insert—

"(4A) Without prejudice to the power to impose conditions given by subsection (3) above, the conditions subject to which a council makes grants, loans or other payments under this section to the governing body of a higher education institution shall require the governing body to publish disability statements at such intervals as may be specified.

(4B) For the purposes of subsection (4A) above—

"disability statement" means a statement containing information of a specified description about the provision of facilities for education and research made by the institution in respect of persons who are disabled persons for the purposes of the Disability Discrimination Act 1995; and

"specified" means specified in the conditions subject to which grants, loans or other payments are made by a council under this section."

(7) The Education Act 1944 is amended as set out in subsections (8) and (9).

PART IV
1944 c. 31.

(8) In section 41 (functions of local education authorities in respect of further education), after subsection (2) insert—

"(2A) It shall be the duty of every local education authority to publish disability statements at such intervals as may be prescribed.

(2B) For the purposes of subsection (2A) above—

"disability statement" means a statement containing information of a prescribed description about the provision of facilities for further education made by the local education authority in respect of persons who are disabled persons for the purposes of the Disability Discrimination Act 1995; and

1995 c. 50.

"prescribed" means prescribed by regulations made by the Secretary of State."

(9) In section 41(7), (8) and (11), for "this section" substitute "subsections (1) and (6) above".

31.—(1) The Further and Higher Education (Scotland) Act 1992 is amended as follows.

Further and higher education of disabled persons: Scotland.
1992 c. 37.

(2) In section 37 (establishment of Scottish Higher Education Funding Council) after subsection (4) insert—

"(4A) In exercising their functions, the Council shall have regard to the requirements of disabled persons.

(4B) In subsection (4A) above, "disabled persons" means persons who are disabled persons for the purpose of the Disability Discrimination Act 1995."

(3) In section 40 (administration of funds by the Council), after subsection (4) insert—

"(5) Without prejudice to the power to impose conditions given by subsection (3) above, the conditions subject to which the Council make grants, loans or other payments under this section to the governing body of an institution within the higher education sector shall require the governing body to publish disability statements at such intervals as may be specified.

(6) For the purposes of subsection (5) above—

"disability statement" means a statement containing information of a specified description about the provision of facilities for education and research made by the institution in respect of persons who are disabled persons for the purpose of the Disability Discrimination Act 1995; and "specified" means specified in the conditions subject to which grants, loans or other payments are made by the Council under this section."

Part V

Public Transport

Taxis

Taxi accessibility regulations.

32.—(1) The Secretary of State may make regulations ("taxi accessibility regulations") for the purpose of securing that it is possible—

(a) for disabled persons—

(i) to get into and out of taxis in safety;

(ii) to be carried in taxis in safety and in reasonable comfort; and

(b) for disabled persons in wheelchairs—

(i) to be conveyed in safety into and out of taxis while remaining in their wheelchairs; and

(ii) to be carried in taxis in safety and in reasonable comfort while remaining in their wheelchairs.

(2) Taxi accessibility regulations may, in particular—

(a) require any regulated taxi to conform with provisions of the regulations as to—

(i) the size of any door opening which is for the use of passengers;

(ii) the floor area of the passenger compartment;

(iii) the amount of headroom in the passenger compartment;

(iv) the fitting of restraining devices designed to ensure the stability of a wheelchair while the taxi is moving;

(b) require the driver of any regulated taxi which is plying for hire, or which has been hired, to comply with provisions of the regulations as to the carrying of ramps or other devices designed to facilitate the loading and unloading of wheelchairs;

(c) require the driver of any regulated taxi in which a disabled person who is in a wheelchair is being carried (while remaining in his wheelchair) to comply with provisions of the regulations as to the position in which the wheelchair is to be secured.

(3) The driver of a regulated taxi which is plying for hire, or which has been hired, is guilty of an offence if—

(a) he fails to comply with any requirement imposed on him by the regulations; or

(b) the taxi fails to conform with any provision of the regulations with which it is required to conform.

(4) A person who is guilty of such an offence is liable, on summary conviction, to a fine not exceeding level 3 on the standard scale.

(5) In this section—

"passenger compartment" has such meaning as may be prescribed;

"regulated taxi" means any taxi to which the regulations are expressed to apply;

"taxi" means a vehicle licensed under—

(a) section 37 of the Town Police Clauses Act 1847, or

(b) section 6 of the Metropolitan Public Carriage Act 1869,

but does not include a taxi which is drawn by a horse or other animal.

1847 c. 89.

1869 c. 115.

33.—(1) In this section "a franchise agreement" means a contract entered into by the operator of a designated transport facility for the provision by the other party to the contract of hire car services—

(a) for members of the public using any part of the transport facility; and

(b) which involve vehicles entering any part of that facility.

Designated transport facilities.

(2) The Secretary of State may by regulations provide for the application of any taxi provision in relation to—

(a) vehicles used for the provision of services under a franchise agreement; or

(b) the drivers of such vehicles.

(3) Any regulations under subsection (2) may apply any taxi provision with such modifications as the Secretary of State considers appropriate.

(4) In this section—

"designated" means designated for the purposes of this section by an order made by the Secretary of State;

"hire car" has such meaning as may be prescribed;

"operator", in relation to a transport facility, means any person who is concerned with the management or operation of the facility;

"taxi provision" means any provision of—

(a) this Act, or

(b) regulations made in pursuance of section 20(2A) of the Civic Government (Scotland) Act 1982,

which applies in relation to taxis or the drivers of taxis; and

1982 c. 45.

"transport facility" means any premises which form part of any port, airport, railway station or bus station.

34.—(1) No licensing authority shall grant a licence for a taxi to ply for hire unless the vehicle conforms with those provisions of the taxi accessibility regulations with which it will be required to conform if licensed.

New licences conditional on compliance with taxi accessibility regulations.

(2) Subsection (1) does not apply if such a licence was in force with respect to the vehicle at any time during the period of 28 days immediately before the day on which the licence is granted.

(3) The Secretary of State may by order provide for subsection (2) to cease to have effect on such date as may be specified in the order.

(4) Separate orders may be made under subsection (3) with respect to different areas or localities.

35.—(1) The Secretary of State may make regulations ("exemption regulations") for the purpose of enabling any relevant licensing authority to apply to him for an order (an "exemption order") exempting the authority from the requirements of section 34.

(2) Exemption regulations may, in particular, make provision requiring a licensing authority proposing to apply for an exemption order—

    (a) to carry out such consultations as may be prescribed;

    (b) to publish the proposal in the prescribed manner;

    (c) to consider any representations made to it about the proposal, before applying for the order;

    (d) to make its application in the prescribed form.

(3) A licensing authority may apply for an exemption order only if it is satisfied—

    (a) that, having regard to the circumstances prevailing in its area, it would be inappropriate for the requirements of section 34 to apply; and

    (b) that the application of section 34 would result in an unacceptable reduction in the number of taxis in its area.

(4) After considering any application for an exemption order and consulting the Disabled Persons Transport Advisory Committee and such other persons as he considers appropriate, the Secretary of State may—

    (a) make an exemption order in the terms of the application;

    (b) make an exemption order in such other terms as he considers appropriate; or

    (c) refuse to make an exemption order.

(5) The Secretary of State may by regulations ("swivel seat regulations") make provision requiring any exempt taxi plying for hire in an area in respect of which an exemption order is in force to conform with provisions of the regulations as to the fitting and use of swivel seats.

(6) The Secretary of State may by regulations make provision with respect to swivel seat regulations similar to that made by section 34 with respect to taxi accessibility regulations.

(7) In this section—

    "exempt taxi" means a taxi in relation to which section 34(1) would apply if the exemption order were not in force;

    "relevant licensing authority" means a licensing authority responsible for licensing taxis in any area of England and Wales other than the area to which the Metropolitan Public Carriage Act 1869 applies; and

    "swivel seats" has such meaning as may be prescribed.

36.—(1) This section imposes duties on the driver of a regulated taxi which has been hired—

    (a) by or for a disabled person who is in a wheelchair; or

    (b) by a person who wishes such a disabled person to accompany him in the taxi.

(2) In this section—

"carry" means carry in the taxi concerned; and

"the passenger" means the disabled person concerned.

(3) The duties are—

(a) to carry the passenger while he remains in his wheelchair;

(b) not to make any additional charge for doing so;

(c) if the passenger chooses to sit in a passenger seat, to carry the wheelchair;

(d) to take such steps as are necessary to ensure that the passenger is carried in safety and in reasonable comfort;

(e) to give such assistance as may be reasonably required—

(i) to enable the passenger to get into or out of the taxi;

(ii) if the passenger wishes to remain in his wheelchair, to enable him to be conveyed into and out of the taxi while in his wheelchair;

(iii) to load the passenger's luggage into or out of the taxi;

(iv) if the passenger does not wish to remain in his wheelchair, to load the wheelchair into or out of the taxi.

(4) Nothing in this section is to be taken to require the driver of any taxi—

(a) except in the case of a taxi of a prescribed description, to carry more than one person in a wheelchair, or more than one wheelchair, on any one journey; or

(b) to carry any person in circumstances in which it would otherwise be lawful for him to refuse to carry that person.

(5) A driver of a regulated taxi who fails to comply with any duty imposed on him by this section is guilty of an offence and liable, on summary conviction, to a fine not exceeding level 3 on the standard scale.

(6) In any proceedings for an offence under this section, it is a defence for the accused to show that, even though at the time of the alleged offence the taxi conformed with those provisions of the taxi accessibility regulations with which it was required to conform, it would not have been possible for the wheelchair in question to be carried in safety in the taxi.

(7) If the licensing authority is satisfied that it is appropriate to exempt a person from the duties imposed by this section—

(a) on medical grounds, or

(b) on the ground that his physical condition makes it impossible or unreasonably difficult for him to comply with the duties imposed on drivers by this section,

it shall issue him with a certificate of exemption.

(8) A certificate of exemption shall be issued for such period as may be specified in the certificate.

(9) The driver of a regulated taxi is exempt from the duties imposed by this section if—

(a) a certificate of exemption issued to him under this section is in force; and

(b) the prescribed notice of his exemption is exhibited on the taxi in the prescribed manner.

Carrying of guide dogs and hearing dogs.

37.—(1) This section imposes duties on the driver of a taxi which has been hired—

(a) by or for a disabled person who is accompanied by his guide dog or hearing dog, or

(b) by a person who wishes such a disabled person to accompany him in the taxi.

(2) The disabled person is referred to in this section as "the passenger".

(3) The duties are—

(a) to carry the passenger's dog and allow it to remain with the passenger; and

(b) not to make any additional charge for doing so.

(4) A driver of a taxi who fails to comply with any duty imposed on him by this section is guilty of an offence and liable, on summary conviction, to a fine not exceeding level 3 on the standard scale.

(5) If the licensing authority is satisfied that it is appropriate on medical grounds to exempt a person from the duties imposed by this section, it shall issue him with a certificate of exemption.

(6) In determining whether to issue a certificate of exemption, the licensing authority shall, in particular, have regard to the physical characteristics of the taxi which the applicant drives or those of any kind of taxi in relation to which he requires the certificate.

(7) A certificate of exemption shall be issued—

(a) with respect to a specified taxi or a specified kind of taxi; and

(b) for such period as may be specified in the certificate.

(8) The driver of a taxi is exempt from the duties imposed by this section if—

(a) a certificate of exemption issued to him under this section is in force with respect to the taxi; and

(b) the prescribed notice of his exemption is exhibited on the taxi in the prescribed manner.

(9) The Secretary of State may, for the purposes of this section, prescribe any other category of dog trained to assist a disabled person who has a disability of a prescribed kind.

(10) This section applies in relation to any such prescribed category of dog as it applies in relation to guide dogs.

(11) In this section—

"guide dog" means a dog which has been trained to guide a blind person; and

"hearing dog" means a dog which has been trained to assist a deaf person.

PART V

Appeal against refusal of exemption certificate.

38.—(1) Any person who is aggrieved by the refusal of a licensing authority to issue an exemption certificate under section 36 or 37 may appeal to the appropriate court before the end of the period of 28 days beginning with the date of the refusal.

(2) On an appeal to it under this section, the court may direct the licensing authority concerned to issue the appropriate certificate of exemption to have effect for such period as may be specified in the direction.

(3) "Appropriate court" means the magistrates' court for the petty sessions area in which the licensing authority has its principal office.

Requirements as to disabled passengers in Scotland.
1982 c. 45.

39.—(1) Part II of the Civic Government (Scotland) Act 1982 (licensing and regulation) is amended as follows.

(2) In subsection (4) of section 10 (suitability of vehicle for use as taxi)—

(a) after "authority" insert "— (a)"; and

(b) at the end add "; and

(b) as not being so suitable if it does not so comply."

(3) In section 20 (regulations relating to taxis etc.) after subsection (2) insert—

"(2A) Without prejudice to the generality of subsections (1) and (2) above, regulations under those subsections may make such provision as appears to the Secretary of State to be necessary or expedient in relation to the carrying in taxis of disabled persons (within the meaning of section 1(2) of the Disability Discrimination Act 1995) and such provision may in particular prescribe—

1995 c. 50.

(a) requirements as to the carriage of wheelchairs, guide dogs, hearing dogs and other categories of dog;

(b) a date from which any such provision is to apply and the extent to which it is to apply; and

(c) the circumstances in which an exemption from such provision may be granted in respect of any taxi or taxi driver,

and in this subsection—

"guide dog" means a dog which has been trained to guide a blind person;

"hearing dog" means a dog which has been trained to assist a deaf person; and

"other categories of dog" means such other categories of dog as the Secretary of State may prescribe, trained to assist disabled persons who have disabilities of such kinds as he may prescribe."

Public service vehicles

PSV accessibility
regulations.

40.—(1) The Secretary of State may make regulations ("PSV accessibility regulations") for the purpose of securing that it is possible for disabled persons—

   (a) to get on to and off regulated public service vehicles in safety and without unreasonable difficulty (and, in the case of disabled persons in wheelchairs, to do so while remaining in their wheelchairs); and

   (b) to be carried in such vehicles in safety and in reasonable comfort.

(2) PSV accessibility regulations may, in particular, make provision as to the construction, use and maintenance of regulated public service vehicles including provision as to—

   (a) the fitting of equipment to vehicles;

   (b) equipment to be carried by vehicles;

   (c) the design of equipment to be fitted to, or carried by, vehicles;

   (d) the fitting and use of restraining devices designed to ensure the stability of wheelchairs while vehicles are moving;

   (e) the position in which wheelchairs are to be secured while vehicles are moving.

(3) Any person who—

   (a) contravenes or fails to comply with any provision of the PSV accessibility regulations,

   (b) uses on a road a regulated public service vehicle which does not conform with any provision of the regulations with which it is required to conform, or

   (c) causes or permits to be used on a road such a regulated public service vehicle,

is guilty of an offence.

(4) A person who is guilty of such an offence is liable, on summary conviction, to a fine not exceeding level 4 on the standard scale.

(5) In this section—

"public service vehicle" means a vehicle which is—

      (a) adapted to carry more than eight passengers; and

1981 c. 14.

      (b) a public service vehicle for the purposes of the Public Passenger Vehicles Act 1981;

"regulated public service vehicle" means any public service vehicle to which the PSV accessibility regulations are expressed to apply.

(6) Different provision may be made in regulations under this section—

   (a) as respects different classes or descriptions of vehicle;

   (b) as respects the same class or description of vehicle in different circumstances.

(7) Before making any regulations under this section or section 41 or 42 the Secretary of State shall consult the Disabled Persons Transport Advisory Committee and such other representative organisations as he thinks fit.

41.—(1) A regulated public service vehicle shall not be used on a road unless—

    (a) a vehicle examiner has issued a certificate (an "accessibility certificate") that such provisions of the PSV accessibility regulations as may be prescribed are satisfied in respect of the vehicle; or

    (b) an approval certificate has been issued under section 42 in respect of the vehicle.

(2) The Secretary of State may make regulations—

    (a) with respect to applications for, and the issue of, accessibility certificates;

    (b) providing for the examination of vehicles in respect of which applications have been made;

    (c) with respect to the issue of copies of accessibility certificates in place of certificates which have been lost or destroyed.

(3) If a regulated public service vehicle is used in contravention of this section, the operator of the vehicle is guilty of an offence and liable on summary conviction to a fine not exceeding level 4 on the standard scale.

(4) In this section "operator" has the same meaning as in the Public Passenger Vehicles Act 1981.

42.—(1) Where the Secretary of State is satisfied that such provisions of the PSV accessibility regulations as may be prescribed for the purposes of section 41 are satisfied in respect of a particular vehicle he may approve the vehicle for the purposes of this section.

(2) A vehicle which has been so approved is referred to in this section as a "type vehicle".

(3) Subsection (4) applies where a declaration in the prescribed form has been made by an authorised person that a particular vehicle conforms in design, construction and equipment with a type vehicle.

(4) A vehicle examiner may, after examining (if he thinks fit) the vehicle to which the declaration applies, issue a certificate in the prescribed form ("an approval certificate") that it conforms to the type vehicle.

(5) The Secretary of State may make regulations—

    (a) with respect to applications for, and grants of, approval under subsection (1);

    (b) with respect to applications for, and the issue of, approval certificates;

    (c) providing for the examination of vehicles in respect of which applications have been made;

    (d) with respect to the issue of copies of approval certificates in place of certificates which have been lost or destroyed.

(6) The Secretary of State may at any time withdraw his approval of a type vehicle.

(7) Where an approval is withdrawn—

    (a) no further approval certificates shall be issued by reference to the type vehicle; but

(b) any approval certificate issued by reference to the type vehicle before the withdrawal shall continue to have effect for the purposes of section 41.

(8) In subsection (3) "authorised person" means a person authorised by the Secretary of State for the purposes of that subsection.

Special authorisations.

43.—(1) The Secretary of State may by order authorise the use on roads of—

(a) any regulated public service vehicle of a class or description specified by the order, or

(b) any regulated public service vehicle which is so specified,

and nothing in section 40, 41 or 42 prevents the use of any vehicle in accordance with the order.

(2) Any such authorisation may be given subject to such restrictions and conditions as may be specified by or under the order.

(3) The Secretary of State may by order make provision for the purpose of securing that, subject to such restrictions and conditions as may be specified by or under the order, provisions of the PSV accessibility regulations apply to regulated public service vehicles of a description specified by the order subject to such modifications or exceptions as may be specified by the order.

Reviews and appeals.

44.—(1) Subsection (2) applies where—

(a) the Secretary of State refuses an application for the approval of a vehicle under section 42(1); and

(b) before the end of the prescribed period, the applicant asks the Secretary of State to review the decision and pays any fee fixed under section 45.

(2) The Secretary of State shall—

(a) review the decision; and

(b) in doing so, consider any representations made to him in writing, before the end of the prescribed period, by the applicant.

(3) A person applying for an accessibility certificate or an approval certificate may appeal to the Secretary of State against the refusal of a vehicle examiner to issue such a certificate.

(4) An appeal must be made within the prescribed time and in the prescribed manner.

(5) Regulations may make provision as to the procedure to be followed in connection with appeals.

(6) On the determination of an appeal, the Secretary of State may—

(a) confirm, vary or reverse the decision appealed against;

(b) give such directions as he thinks fit to the vehicle examiner for giving effect to his decision.

Fees.

45.—(1) Such fees, payable at such times, as may be prescribed may be charged by the Secretary of State in respect of—

(a) applications for, and grants of, approval under section 42(1);

(b) applications for, and the issue of, accessibility certificates and approval certificates;

(c) copies of such certificates;

(d) reviews and appeals under section 44.

(2) Any such fees received by the Secretary of State shall be paid by him into the Consolidated Fund.

(3) Regulations under subsection (1) may make provision for the repayment of fees, in whole or in part, in such circumstances as may be prescribed.

(4) Before making any regulations under subsection (1) the Secretary of State shall consult such representative organisations as he thinks fit.

Rail vehicles

46.—(1) The Secretary of State may make regulations ("rail vehicle accessibility regulations") for the purpose of securing that it is possible— Rail vehicle accessibility regulations.

(a) for disabled persons—

(i) to get on to and off regulated rail vehicles in safety and without unreasonable difficulty;

(ii) to be carried in such vehicles in safety and in reasonable comfort; and

(b) for disabled persons in wheelchairs—

(i) to get on to and off such vehicles in safety and without unreasonable difficulty while remaining in their wheelchairs, and

(ii) to be carried in such vehicles in safety and in reasonable comfort while remaining in their wheelchairs.

(2) Rail vehicle accessibility regulations may, in particular, make provision as to the construction, use and maintenance of regulated rail vehicles including provision as to—

(a) the fitting of equipment to vehicles;

(b) equipment to be carried by vehicles;

(c) the design of equipment to be fitted to, or carried by, vehicles;

(d) the use of equipment fitted to, or carried by, vehicles;

(e) the toilet facilities to be provided in vehicles;

(f) the location and floor area of the wheelchair accommodation to be provided in vehicles;

(g) assistance to be given to disabled persons.

(3) If a regulated rail vehicle which does not conform with any provision of the rail vehicle accessibility regulations with which it is required to conform is used for carriage, the operator of the vehicle is guilty of an offence.

(4) A person who is guilty of such an offence is liable, on summary conviction, to a fine not exceeding level 4 on the standard scale.

(5) Different provision may be made in rail vehicle accessibility regulations—

(a) as respects different classes or descriptions of rail vehicle;

(b) as respects the same class or description of rail vehicle in different circumstances;

(c) as respects different networks.

(6) In this section—

"network" means any permanent way or other means of guiding or supporting rail vehicles or any section of it;

"operator", in relation to any rail vehicle, means the person having the management of that vehicle;

"rail vehicle" means a vehicle—

(a) constructed or adapted to carry passengers on any railway, tramway or prescribed system; and

(b) first brought into use, or belonging to a class of vehicle first brought into use, after 31st December 1998;

"regulated rail vehicle" means any rail vehicle to which the rail vehicle accessibility regulations are expressed to apply; and

"wheelchair accommodation" has such meaning as may be prescribed.

(7) In subsection (6)—

"prescribed system" means a system using a prescribed mode of guided transport ("guided transport" having the same meaning as in the Transport and Works Act 1992); and

1992 c. 42.

"railway" and "tramway" have the same meaning as in that Act.

(8) The Secretary of State may by regulations make provision as to the time when a rail vehicle, or a class of rail vehicle, is to be treated, for the purposes of this section, as first brought into use.

(9) Regulations under subsection (8) may include provision for disregarding periods of testing and other prescribed periods of use.

(10) For the purposes of this section and section 47, a person uses a vehicle for carriage if he uses it for the carriage of members of the public for hire or reward at separate fares.

(11) Before making any regulations under subsection (1) or section 47 the Secretary of State shall consult the Disabled Persons Transport Advisory Committee and such other representative organisations as he thinks fit.

Exemption from rail vehicle accessibility regulations.

47.—(1) The Secretary of State may by order (an "exemption order") authorise the use for carriage of any regulated rail vehicle of a specified description, or in specified circumstances, even though that vehicle does not conform with the provisions of the rail vehicle accessibility regulations with which it is required to conform.

(2) Regulations may make provision with respect to exemption orders including, in particular, provision as to—

(a) the persons by whom applications for exemption orders may be made;

(b) the form in which such applications are to be made;

(c) information to be supplied in connection with such applications;

(d) the period for which exemption orders are to continue in force;

(e) the revocation of exemption orders.

(3) After considering any application for an exemption order and consulting the Disabled Persons Transport Advisory Committee and such other persons as he considers appropriate, the Secretary of State may—

(a) make an exemption order in the terms of the application;

(b) make an exemption order in such other terms as he considers appropriate;

(c) refuse to make an exemption order.

(4) An exemption order may be made subject to such restrictions and conditions as may be specified.

(5) In this section "specified" means specified in an exemption order.

Supplemental

48.—(1) Where an offence under section 40 or 46 committed by a body corporate is committed with the consent or connivance of, or is attributable to any neglect on the part of, a director, manager, secretary or other similar officer of the body, or a person purporting to act in such a capacity, he as well as the body corporate is guilty of the offence.

Offences by bodies corporate etc.

(2) In subsection (1) "director", in relation to a body corporate whose affairs are managed by its members, means a member of the body corporate.

(3) Where, in Scotland, an offence under section 40 or 46 committed by a partnership or by an unincorporated association other than a partnership is committed with the consent or connivance of, or is attributable to any neglect on the part of, a partner in the partnership or (as the case may be) a person concerned in the management or control of the association, he, as well as the partnership or association, is guilty of the offence.

49.—(1) In this section "relevant document" means—

Forgery and false statements.

(a) a certificate of exemption issued under section 36 or 37;

(b) a notice of a kind mentioned in section 36(9)(b) or 37(8)(b);

(c) an accessibility certificate; or

(d) an approval certificate.

(2) A person is guilty of an offence if, with intent to deceive, he—

(a) forges, alters or uses a relevant document;

(b) lends a relevant document to any other person;

(c) allows a relevant document to be used by any other person; or

(d) makes or has in his possession any document which closely resembles a relevant document.

(3) A person who is guilty of an offence under subsection (2) is liable—

(a) on summary conviction, to a fine not exceeding the statutory maximum;

(b) on conviction on indictment, to imprisonment for a term not exceeding two years or to a fine or to both.

(4) A person who knowingly makes a false statement for the purpose of obtaining an accessibility certificate or an approval certificate is guilty of an offence and liable on summary conviction to a fine not exceeding level 4 on the standard scale.

PART VI

THE NATIONAL DISABILITY COUNCIL

The National
Disability
Council.

50.—(1) There shall be a body to be known as the National Disability Council (but in this Act referred to as "the Council").

(2) It shall be the duty of the Council to advise the Secretary of State, either on its own initiative or when asked to do so by the Secretary of State—

    (a) on matters relevant to the elimination of discrimination against disabled persons and persons who have had a disability;

    (b) on measures which are likely to reduce or eliminate such discrimination; and

    (c) on matters related to the operation of this Act or of provisions made under this Act.

(3) The Secretary of State may by order confer additional functions on the Council.

(4) The power conferred by subsection (3) does not include power to confer on the Council any functions with respect to the investigation of any complaint which may be the subject of proceedings under this Act.

(5) In discharging its duties under this section, the Council shall in particular have regard to—

    (a) the extent and nature of the benefits which would be likely to result from the implementation of any recommendation which it makes; and

    (b) the likely cost of implementing any such recommendation.

(6) Where the Council makes any recommendation in the discharge of any of its functions under this section it shall, if it is reasonably practicable to do so, make an assessment of—

    (a) the likely cost of implementing the recommendation; and

    (b) the likely financial benefits which would result from implementing it.

(7) Where the Council proposes to give the Secretary of State advice on a matter, it shall before doing so—

    (a) consult any body—

        (i) established by any enactment or by a Minister of the Crown for the purpose of giving advice in relation to disability, or any aspect of disability; and

        (ii) having functions in relation to the matter to which the advice relates;

    (b) consult such other persons as it considers appropriate; and

    (c) have regard to any representations made to it as a result of any such consultations.

(8) Schedule 5 makes further provision with respect to the Council, including provision about its membership.

(9) The power conferred on the Council by subsection (2) to give advice on its own initiative does not include power to give advice—

(a) by virtue of paragraph (a) or (b), in respect of any matter which relates to the operation of any provision of or arrangements made under—

(i) the Disabled Persons (Employment) Acts 1944 and 1958;

(ii) the Employment and Training Act 1973;

(iii) the Employment Protection (Consolidation) Act 1978; or

(iv) section 2(3) of the Enterprise and New Towns (Scotland) Act 1990; or

(b) by virtue of paragraph (c), in respect of any matter arising under Part II or section 53, 54, 56 or 61.

1944 c. 10.
1958 c. 33.
1973 c. 50.
1978 c. 44.
1990 c. 35.

(10) Subsection (9) shall not have effect at any time when there is neither a national advisory council established under section 17(1)(a) of the Disabled Persons (Employment) Act 1944 nor any person appointed to act generally under section 60(1) of this Act.

51.—(1) It shall be the duty of the Council, when asked to do so by the Secretary of State—

(a) to prepare proposals for a code of practice dealing with the matters to which the Secretary of State's request relates; or

(b) to review a code and, if it considers it appropriate, propose alterations.

Codes of practice prepared by the Council.

(2) The Secretary of State may, in accordance with the procedural provisions of section 52, issue codes of practice in response to proposals made by the Council under this section.

(3) A failure on the part of any person to observe any provision of a code does not of itself make that person liable to any proceedings.

(4) A code is admissible in evidence in any proceedings under this Act before an industrial tribunal, a county court or a sheriff court.

(5) If any provision of a code appears to a tribunal or court to be relevant to any question arising in any proceedings under this Act, it shall be taken into account in determining that question.

(6) In this section and section 52 "code" means a code issued by the Secretary of State under this section and includes a code which has been altered and re-issued.

52.—(1) In this section "proposal" means a proposal made by the Council to the Secretary of State under section 51.

Further provision about codes issued under section 51.

(2) In preparing any proposal, the Council shall consult—

(a) such persons (if any) as the Secretary of State has specified in making his request to the Council; and

(b) such other persons (if any) as the Council considers appropriate.

PART VI

(3) Before making any proposal, the Council shall publish a draft, consider any representations made to it about the draft and, if it thinks it appropriate, modify its proposal in the light of any of those representations.

(4) Where the Council makes any proposal, the Secretary of State may—

(a) approve it;

(b) approve it subject to such modifications as he considers appropriate; or

(c) refuse to approve it.

(5) Where the Secretary of State approves any proposal (with or without modifications), he shall prepare a draft of the proposed code and lay it before each House of Parliament.

(6) If, within the 40-day period, either House resolves not to approve the draft, the Secretary of State shall take no further steps in relation to the proposed code.

(7) If no such resolution is made within the 40-day period, the Secretary of State shall issue the code in the form of his draft.

(8) The code shall come into force on such date as the Secretary of State may appoint by order.

(9) Subsection (6) does not prevent a new draft of the proposed code from being laid before Parliament.

(10) If the Secretary of State refuses to approve a proposal, he shall give the Council a written statement of his reasons for not approving it.

(11) The Secretary of State may by order revoke a code.

(12) In this section "40-day period", in relation to the draft of a proposed code, means—

(a) if the draft is laid before one House on a day later than the day on which it is laid before the other House, the period of 40 days beginning with the later of the two days, and

(b) in any other case, the period of 40 days beginning with the day on which the draft is laid before each House,

no account being taken of any period during which Parliament is dissolved or prorogued or during which both Houses are adjourned for more than four days.

PART VII

SUPPLEMENTAL

Codes of practice prepared by the Secretary of State.

53.—(1) The Secretary of State may issue codes of practice containing such practical guidance as he considers appropriate with a view to—

(a) eliminating discrimination in the field of employment against disabled persons and persons who have had a disability; or

(b) encouraging good practice in relation to the employment of disabled persons and persons who have had a disability.

(2) The Secretary of State may from time to time revise the whole or any part of a code and re-issue it.

(3) Without prejudice to subsection (1), a code may include practical guidance as to—

 (a) the circumstances in which it would be reasonable, having regard in particular to the costs involved, for a person to be expected to make adjustments in favour of a disabled person or a person who has had a disability; or

 (b) what steps it is reasonably practicable for employers to take for the purpose of preventing their employees from doing, in the course of their employment, anything which is made unlawful by this Act.

(4) A failure on the part of any person to observe any provision of a code does not of itself make that person liable to any proceedings.

(5) A code is admissible in evidence in any proceedings under this Act before an industrial tribunal, a county court or a sheriff court.

(6) If any provision of a code appears to a tribunal or court to be relevant to any question arising in any proceedings under this Act, it shall be taken into account in determining that question.

(7) In this section and section 54 "code" means a code issued by the Secretary of State under this section and includes a code which has been revised and re-issued.

(8) In subsection (1)(a), "discrimination in the field of employment" includes discrimination of a kind mentioned in section 12 or 13.

(9) In subsections (1)(b) and (3), "employment" includes contract work (as defined by section 12(6)).

54.—(1) In preparing a draft of any code under section 53, the Secretary of State shall consult such organisations representing the interests of employers or of disabled persons in, or seeking, employment as he considers appropriate.

Further provision about codes issued under section 53.

(2) Where the Secretary of State proposes to issue a code, he shall publish a draft of it, consider any representations that are made to him about the draft and, if he thinks it appropriate, modify his proposals in the light of any of those representations.

(3) If the Secretary of State decides to proceed with a proposed code, he shall lay a draft of it before each House of Parliament.

(4) If, within the 40-day period, either House resolves not to approve the draft, the Secretary of State shall take no further steps in relation to the proposed code.

(5) If no such resolution is made within the 40-day period, the Secretary of State shall issue the code in the form of his draft.

(6) The code shall come into force on such date as the Secretary of State may appoint by order.

(7) Subsection (4) does not prevent a new draft of the proposed code from being laid before Parliament.

(8) The Secretary of State may by order revoke a code.

(9) In this section "40-day period", in relation to the draft of a proposed code, means—

(a) if the draft is laid before one House on a day later than the day on which it is laid before the other House, the period of 40 days beginning with the later of the two days, and

(b) in any other case, the period of 40 days beginning with the day on which the draft is laid before each House,

no account being taken of any period during which Parliament is dissolved or prorogued or during which both Houses are adjourned for more than four days.

Victimisation.

55.—(1) For the purposes of Part II or Part III, a person ("A") discriminates against another person ("B") if—

(a) he treats B less favourably than he treats or would treat other persons whose circumstances are the same as B's; and

(b) he does so for a reason mentioned in subsection (2).

(2) The reasons are that—

(a) B has—

(i) brought proceedings against A or any other person under this Act; or

(ii) given evidence or information in connection with such proceedings brought by any person; or

(iii) otherwise done anything under this Act in relation to A or any other person; or

(iv) alleged that A or any other person has (whether or not the allegation so states) contravened this Act; or

(b) A believes or suspects that B has done or intends to do any of those things.

(3) Where B is a disabled person, or a person who has had a disability, the disability in question shall be disregarded in comparing his circumstances with those of any other person for the purposes of subsection (1)(a).

(4) Subsection (1) does not apply to treatment of a person because of an allegation made by him if the allegation was false and not made in good faith.

Help for persons suffering discrimination.

56.—(1) For the purposes of this section—

(a) a person who considers that he may have been discriminated against, in contravention of any provision of Part II, is referred to as "the complainant"; and

(b) a person against whom the complainant may decide to make, or has made, a complaint under Part II is referred to as "the respondent".

(2) The Secretary of State shall, with a view to helping the complainant to decide whether to make a complaint against the respondent and, if he does so, to formulate and present his case in the most effective manner, by order prescribe—

(a) forms by which the complainant may question the respondent on his reasons for doing any relevant act, or on any other matter which is or may be relevant; and

    (b) forms by which the respondent may if he so wishes reply to any questions.

(3) Where the complainant questions the respondent in accordance with forms prescribed by an order under subsection (2)—

    (a) the question, and any reply by the respondent (whether in accordance with such an order or not), shall be admissible as evidence in any proceedings under Part II;

    (b) if it appears to the tribunal in any such proceedings—

        (i) that the respondent deliberately, and without reasonable excuse, omitted to reply within a reasonable period, or

        (ii) that the respondent's reply is evasive or equivocal,

    it may draw any inference which it considers it just and equitable to draw, including an inference that the respondent has contravened a provision of Part II.

(4) The Secretary of State may by order prescribe—

    (a) the period within which questions must be duly served in order to be admissible under subsection (3)(a); and

    (b) the manner in which a question, and any reply by the respondent, may be duly served.

(5) This section is without prejudice to any other enactment or rule of law regulating interlocutory and preliminary matters in proceedings before an industrial tribunal, and has effect subject to any enactment or rule of law regulating the admissibility of evidence in such proceedings.

57.—(1) A person who knowingly aids another person to do an act made unlawful by this Act is to be treated for the purposes of this Act as himself doing the same kind of unlawful act.

    Aiding unlawful acts.

(2) For the purposes of subsection (1), an employee or agent for whose act the employer or principal is liable under section 58 (or would be so liable but for section 58(5)) shall be taken to have aided the employer or principal to do the act.

(3) For the purposes of this section, a person does not knowingly aid another to do an unlawful act if—

    (a) he acts in reliance on a statement made to him by that other person that, because of any provision of this Act, the act would not be unlawful; and

    (b) it is reasonable for him to rely on the statement.

(4) A person who knowingly or recklessly makes such a statement which is false or misleading in a material respect is guilty of an offence.

(5) Any person guilty of an offence under subsection (4) shall be liable on summary conviction to a fine not exceeding level 5 on the standard scale.

58.—(1) Anything done by a person in the course of his employment shall be treated for the purposes of this Act as also done by his employer, whether or not it was done with the employer's knowledge or approval.

    Liability of employers and principals.

PART VII

(2) Anything done by a person as agent for another person with the authority of that other person shall be treated for the purposes of this Act as also done by that other person.

(3) Subsection (2) applies whether the authority was—

(a) express or implied; or

(b) given before or after the act in question was done.

(4) Subsections (1) and (2) do not apply in relation to an offence under section 57(4).

(5) In proceedings under this Act against any person in respect of an act alleged to have been done by an employee of his, it shall be a defence for that person to prove that he took such steps as were reasonably practicable to prevent the employee from—

(a) doing that act; or

(b) doing, in the course of his employment, acts of that description.

Statutory authority and national security etc.

59.—(1) Nothing in this Act makes unlawful any act done—

(a) in pursuance of any enactment; or

(b) in pursuance of any instrument made by a Minister of the Crown under any enactment; or

(c) to comply with any condition or requirement imposed by a Minister of the Crown (whether before or after the passing of this Act) by virtue of any enactment.

(2) In subsection (1) "enactment" includes one passed or made after the date on which this Act is passed and "instrument" includes one made after that date.

(3) Nothing in this Act makes unlawful any act done for the purpose of safeguarding national security.

PART VIII

MISCELLANEOUS

Appointment by Secretary of State of advisers.

60.—(1) The Secretary of State may appoint such persons as he thinks fit to advise or assist him in connection with matters relating to the employment of disabled persons and persons who have had a disability.

(2) Persons may be appointed by the Secretary of State to act generally or in relation to a particular area or locality.

(3) The Secretary of State may pay to any person appointed under this section such allowances and compensation for loss of earnings as he considers appropriate.

(4) The approval of the Treasury is required for any payment under this section.

(5) In subsection (1) "employment" includes self-employment.

(6) The Secretary of State may by order—

(a) provide for section 17 of, and Schedule 2 to, the Disabled Persons (Employment) Act 1944 (national advisory council and district advisory committees) to cease to have effect—

1944 c. 10.

      (i) so far as concerns the national advisory council; or

      (ii) so far as concerns district advisory committees; or

(b) repeal that section and Schedule.

(7) At any time before the coming into force of an order under paragraph (b) of subsection (6), section 17 of the Act of 1944 shall have effect as if in subsection (1), after "disabled persons" in each case there were inserted ", and persons who have had a disability," and as if at the end of the section there were added—

    "(3) For the purposes of this section—

      (a) a person is a disabled person if he is a disabled person for the purposes of the Disability Discrimination Act 1995; and

      (b) "disability" has the same meaning as in that Act."

1995 c. 50.

(8) At any time before the coming into force of an order under paragraph (a)(i) or (b) of subsection (6), section 16 of the Chronically Sick and Disabled Persons Act 1970 (which extends the functions of the national advisory council) shall have effect as if after "disabled persons" in each case there were inserted ", and persons who have had a disability," and as if at the end of the section there were added—

1970 c. 44.

    "(2) For the purposes of this section—

      (a) a person is a disabled person if he is a disabled person for the purposes of the Disability Discrimination Act 1995; and

      (b) "disability" has the same meaning as in that Act."

61.—(1) Section 15 of the Disabled Persons (Employment) Act 1944 (which gives the Secretary of State power to make arrangements for the provision of supported employment) is amended as set out in subsections (2) to (5).

Amendment of Disabled Persons (Employment) Act 1944.
1944 c. 10.

(2) In subsection (1)—

      (a) for "persons registered as handicapped by disablement" substitute "disabled persons";

      (b) for "their disablement" substitute "their disability"; and

      (c) for "are not subject to disablement" substitute "do not have a disability".

(3) In subsection (2), for the words from "any of one or more companies" to "so required and prohibited" substitute "any company, association or body".

(4) After subsection (2) insert—

    "(2A) The only kind of company which the Minister himself may form in exercising his powers under this section is a company which is—

      (a) required by its constitution to apply its profits, if any, or other income in promoting its objects; and

      (b) prohibited by its constitution from paying any dividend to its members."

(5) After subsection (5) insert—

"(5A) For the purposes of this section—

> (a) a person is a disabled person if he is a disabled person for the purposes of the Disability Discrimination Act 1995; and

> (b) "disability" has the same meaning as in that Act."

(6) The provisions of section 16 (preference to be given under section 15 of that Act to ex-service men and women) shall become subsection (1) of that section and at the end insert—

"and whose disability is due to that service.

> (2) For the purposes of subsection (1) of this section, a disabled person's disability shall be treated as due to service of a particular kind only in such circumstances as may be prescribed."

(7) The following provisions of the Act of 1944 shall cease to have effect—

> (a) section 1 (definition of "disabled person");

> (b) sections 6 to 8 (the register of disabled persons);

> (c) sections 9 to 11 (obligations on employers with substantial staffs to employ a quota of registered persons);

> (d) section 12 (the designated employment scheme for persons registered as handicapped by disablement);

> (e) section 13 (interpretation of provisions repealed by this Act);

> (f) section 14 (records to be kept by employers);

> (g) section 19 (proceedings in relation to offences); and

> (h) section 21 (application as respects place of employment, and nationality).

(8) Any provision of subordinate legislation in which "disabled person" is defined by reference to the Act of 1944 shall be construed as if that expression had the same meaning as in this Act.

(9) Subsection (8) does not prevent the further amendment of any such provision by subordinate legislation.

Restriction of publicity: industrial tribunals.

62.—(1) This section applies to proceedings on a complaint under section 8 in which evidence of a personal nature is likely to be heard by the industrial tribunal hearing the complaint.

(2) The power of the Secretary of State to make regulations with respect to the procedure of industrial tribunals includes power to make provision in relation to proceedings to which this section applies for—

> (a) enabling an industrial tribunal, on the application of the complainant or of its own motion, to make a restricted reporting order having effect (if not revoked earlier) until the promulgation of the tribunal's decision; and

> (b) where a restricted reporting order is made in relation to a complaint which is being dealt with by the tribunal together with any other proceedings, enabling the tribunal to direct that the order is to apply also in relation to those other proceedings or such part of them as the tribunal may direct.

(3) If any identifying matter is published or included in a relevant programme in contravention of a restricted reporting order—

(a) in the case of publication in a newspaper or periodical, any proprietor, any editor and any publisher of the newspaper or periodical,

(b) in the case of publication in any other form, the person publishing the matter, and

(c) in the case of matter included in a relevant programme—

    (i) any body corporate engaged in providing the service in which the programme is included, and

    (ii) any person having functions in relation to the programme corresponding to those of an editor of a newspaper,

shall be guilty of an offence and liable on summary conviction to a fine not exceeding level 5 on the standard scale.

(4) Where a person is charged with an offence under subsection (3), it is a defence to prove that at the time of the alleged offence—

(a) he was not aware, and

(b) he neither suspected nor had reason to suspect,

that the publication or programme in question was of, or included, the matter in question.

(5) Where an offence under subsection (3) committed by a body corporate is proved to have been committed with the consent or connivance of, or to be attributable to any neglect on the part of—

(a) a director, manager, secretary or other similar officer of the body corporate, or

(b) a person purporting to act in any such capacity,

he as well as the body corporate is guilty of the offence and liable to be proceeded against and punished accordingly.

(6) In relation to a body corporate whose affairs are managed by its members "director", in subsection (5), means a member of the body corporate.

(7) In this section—

"evidence of a personal nature" means any evidence of a medical, or other intimate, nature which might reasonably be assumed to be likely to cause significant embarrassment to the complainant if reported;

"identifying matter" means any matter likely to lead members of the public to identify the complainant or such other persons (if any) as may be named in the order;

"promulgation" has such meaning as may be prescribed by the regulations;

"relevant programme" means a programme included in a programme service, within the meaning of the Broadcasting Act 1990;   1990 c. 42.

"restricted reporting order" means an order—

    (a) made in exercise of the power conferred by regulations made by virtue of this section; and

(b) prohibiting the publication in Great Britain of identifying matter in a written publication available to the public or its inclusion in a relevant programme for reception in Great Britain; and

"written publication" includes a film, a soundtrack and any other record in permanent form but does not include an indictment or other document prepared for use in particular legal proceedings.

Restriction of publicity: Employment Appeal Tribunal.

63.—(1) This section applies to proceedings—

(a) on an appeal against a decision of an industrial tribunal to make, or not to make, a restricted reporting order, or

(b) on an appeal against any interlocutory decision of an industrial tribunal in proceedings in which the industrial tribunal has made a restricted reporting order which it has not revoked.

(2) The power of the Lord Chancellor to make rules with respect to the procedure of the Employment Appeal Tribunal includes power to make provision in relation to proceedings to which this section applies for—

(a) enabling the Tribunal, on the application of the complainant or of its own motion, to make a restricted reporting order having effect (if not revoked earlier) until the promulgation of the Tribunal's decision; and

(b) where a restricted reporting order is made in relation to an appeal which is being dealt with by the Tribunal together with any other proceedings, enabling the Tribunal to direct that the order is to apply also in relation to those other proceedings or such part of them as the Tribunal may direct.

(3) Subsections (3) to (6) of section 62 apply in relation to a restricted reporting order made by the Tribunal as they apply in relation to one made by an industrial tribunal.

(4) In subsection (1), "restricted reporting order" means an order which is a restricted reporting order for the purposes of section 62.

(5) In subsection (2), "restricted reporting order" means an order—

(a) made in exercise of the power conferred by rules made by virtue of this section; and

(b) prohibiting the publication in Great Britain of identifying matter in a written publication available to the public or its inclusion in a relevant programme for reception in Great Britain.

(6) In this section—

"complainant" means the person who made the complaint to which the proceedings before the Tribunal relate;

"identifying matter", "written publication" and "relevant programme" have the same meaning as in section 62; and

"promulgation" has such meaning as may be prescribed by the rules.

Application to Crown etc.

64.—(1) This Act applies—

(a) to an act done by or for purposes of a Minister of the Crown or government department, or

    (b) to an act done on behalf of the Crown by a statutory body, or a person holding a statutory office,

as it applies to an act done by a private person.

    (2) Subject to subsection (5), Part II applies to service—

    (a) for purposes of a Minister of the Crown or government department, other than service of a person holding a statutory office, or

    (b) on behalf of the Crown for purposes of a person holding a statutory office or purposes of a statutory body,

as it applies to employment by a private person.

    (3) The provisions of Parts II to IV of the 1947 Act apply to proceedings against the Crown under this Act as they apply to Crown proceedings in England and Wales; but section 20 of that Act (removal of proceedings from county court to High Court) does not apply.

    (4) The provisions of Part V of the 1947 Act apply to proceedings against the Crown under this Act as they apply to proceedings in Scotland which by virtue of that Part are treated as civil proceedings by or against the Crown; but the proviso to section 44 of that Act (removal of proceedings from the sheriff court to the Court of Session) does not apply.

    (5) Part II does not apply to service—

    (a) as a member of the Ministry of Defence Police, the British Transport Police, the Royal Parks Constabulary or the United Kingdom Atomic Energy Authority Constabulary;

    (b) as a prison officer; or

    (c) for purposes of a Minister of the Crown or government department having functions with respect to defence as a person who is or may be required by his terms of service to engage in fire fighting.

    (6) Part II does not apply to service as a member of a fire brigade who is or may be required by his terms of service to engage in fire fighting.

    (7) It is hereby declared (for the avoidance of doubt) that Part II does not apply to service in any of the naval, military or air forces of the Crown.

    (8) In this section—

    "the 1947 Act" means the Crown Proceedings Act 1947;   1947 c. 44.

    "British Transport Police" means the constables appointed, or deemed to have been appointed, under section 53 of the British   1949 c. xxix. Transport Commission Act 1949;

    "Crown proceedings" means proceedings which, by virtue of section 23 of the 1947 Act, are treated for the purposes of Part II of that Act as civil proceedings by or against the Crown;

    "fire brigade" means a fire brigade maintained in pursuance of the Fire Services Act 1947;   1947 c. 41.

    "Ministry of Defence Police" means the force established under section 1 of the Ministry of Defence Police Act 1987;   1987 c. 4.

"prison officer" means a person who is a prison officer within the meaning of section 127 of the Criminal Justice and Public Order Act 1994, apart from those who are custody officers within the meaning of Part I of that Act;

"Royal Parks Constabulary" means the park constables appointed under the Parks Regulation Act 1872;

"service for purposes of a Minister of the Crown or government department" does not include service in any office for the time being mentioned in Schedule 2 (Ministerial offices) to the House of Commons Disqualification Act 1975;

"statutory body" means a body set up by or under an enactment;

"statutory office" means an office so set up; and

"United Kingdom Atomic Energy Authority Constabulary" means the special constables appointed under section 3 of the Special Constables Act 1923 on the nomination of the United Kingdom Atomic Energy Authority.

65.—(1) This Act applies to an act done by or for purposes of the House of Lords or the House of Commons as it applies to an act done by a private person.

(2) For the purposes of the application of Part II in relation to the House of Commons, the Corporate Officer of that House shall be treated as the employer of a person who is (or would be) a relevant member of the House of Commons staff for the purposes of section 139 of the Employment Protection (Consolidation) Act 1978.

(3) Except as provided in subsection (4), for the purposes of the application of sections 19 to 21, the provider of services is—

(a) as respects the House of Lords, the Corporate Officer of that House; and

(b) as respects the House of Commons, the Corporate Officer of that House.

(4) Where the service in question is access to and use of any place in the Palace of Westminster which members of the public are permitted to enter, the Corporate Officers of both Houses jointly are the provider of that service.

(5) Nothing in any rule of law or the law or practice of Parliament prevents proceedings being instituted before an industrial tribunal under Part II or before any court under Part III.

66.—(1) Subject to regulations under subsection (3), this section applies to any appointment made by a Minister of the Crown or government department to an office or post where Part II does not apply in relation to the appointment.

(2) In making the appointment, and in making arrangements for determining to whom the office or post should be offered, the Minister of the Crown or government department shall not act in a way which would contravene Part II if he or the department were the employer for the purposes of this Act.

(3) Regulations may provide for this section not to apply to such appointments as may be prescribed.

67.—(1) Any power under this Act to make regulations or orders shall be exercisable by statutory instrument.

(2) Any such power may be exercised to make different provision for different cases, including different provision for different areas or localities.

(3) Any such power includes power—

(a) to make such incidental, supplemental, consequential or transitional provision as appears to the Secretary of State to be expedient; and

(b) to provide for a person to exercise a discretion in dealing with any matter.

(4) No order shall be made under section 50(3) unless a draft of the statutory instrument containing the order has been laid before Parliament and approved by a resolution of each House.

(5) Any other statutory instrument made under this Act, other than one made under section 3(9), 52(8), 54(6) or 70(3), shall be subject to annulment in pursuance of a resolution of either House of Parliament.

(6) Subsection (1) does not require an order under section 43 which applies only to a specified vehicle, or to vehicles of a specified person, to be made by statutory instrument but such an order shall be as capable of being amended or revoked as an order which is made by statutory instrument.

(7) Nothing in section 34(4), 40(6) or 46(5) affects the powers conferred by subsections (2) and (3).

68.—(1) In this Act—

Interpretation.

"accessibility certificate" means a certificate issued under section 41(1)(a);

"act" includes a deliberate omission;

"approval certificate" means a certificate issued under section 42(4);

"benefits", in Part II, has the meaning given in section 4(4);

"conciliation officer" means a person designated under section 211 of the Trade Union and Labour Relations (Consolidation) Act 1992;

1992 c. 52.

"employment" means, subject to any prescribed provision, employment under a contract of service or of apprenticeship or a contract personally to do any work, and related expressions are to be construed accordingly;

"employment at an establishment in Great Britain" is to be construed in accordance with subsections (2) to (5);

"enactment" includes subordinate legislation and any Order in Council;

"licensing authority" means—

(a) in relation to the area to which the Metropolitan Public Carriage Act 1869 applies, the Secretary of State or the holder of any office for the time being designated by the Secretary of State; or

1869 c. 115.

(b) in relation to any other area in England and Wales, the authority responsible for licensing taxis in that area;

PART VIII

1983 c. 20.
1984 c. 36.

"mental impairment" does not have the same meaning as in the Mental Health Act 1983 or the Mental Health (Scotland) Act 1984 but the fact that an impairment would be a mental impairment for the purposes of either of those Acts does not prevent it from being a mental impairment for the purposes of this Act;

"Minister of the Crown" includes the Treasury;

1993 c. 48.

"occupational pension scheme" has the same meaning as in the Pension Schemes Act 1993;

"premises" includes land of any description;

"prescribed" means prescribed by regulations;

"profession" includes any vocation or occupation;

"provider of services" has the meaning given in section 19(2)(b);

"public service vehicle" and "regulated public service vehicle" have the meaning given in section 40;

"PSV accessibility regulations" means regulations made under section 40(1);

"rail vehicle" and "regulated rail vehicle" have the meaning given in section 46;

"rail vehicle accessibility regulations" means regulations made under section 46(1);

"regulations" means regulations made by the Secretary of State;

"section 6 duty" means any duty imposed by or under section 6;

"section 15 duty" means any duty imposed by or under section 15;

"section 21 duty" means any duty imposed by or under section 21;

1978 c. 30.

"subordinate legislation" has the same meaning as in section 21 of the Interpretation Act 1978;

"taxi" and "regulated taxi" have the meaning given in section 32;

"taxi accessibility regulations" means regulations made under section 32(1);

"trade" includes any business;

"trade organisation" has the meaning given in section 13;

1988 c. 52.

"vehicle examiner" means an examiner appointed under section 66A of the Road Traffic Act 1988.

(2) Where an employee does his work wholly or mainly outside Great Britain, his employment is not to be treated as being work at an establishment in Great Britain even if he does some of his work at such an establishment.

(3) Except in prescribed cases, employment on board a ship, aircraft or hovercraft is to be regarded as not being employment at an establishment in Great Britain.

(4) Employment of a prescribed kind, or in prescribed circumstances, is to be regarded as not being employment at an establishment in Great Britain.

(5) Where work is not done at an establishment it shall be treated as done—

    (a) at the establishment from which it is done; or

(b) where it is not done from any establishment, at the establishment with which it has the closest connection.

69. There shall be paid out of money provided by Parliament—

(a) any expenditure incurred by a Minister of the Crown under this Act;

(b) any increase attributable to this Act in the sums payable out of money so provided under or by virtue of any other enactment.

70.—(1) This Act may be cited as the Disability Discrimination Act 1995.

(2) This section (apart from subsections (4), (5) and (7)) comes into force on the passing of this Act.

(3) The other provisions of this Act come into force on such day as the Secretary of State may by order appoint and different days may be appointed for different purposes.

(4) Schedule 6 makes consequential amendments.

(5) The repeals set out in Schedule 7 shall have effect.

(6) This Act extends to Northern Ireland, but in their application to Northern Ireland the provisions of this Act mentioned in Schedule 8 shall have effect subject to the modifications set out in that Schedule.

(7) In Part II of Schedule 1 to the House of Commons Disqualification Act 1975 and in Part II of Schedule 1 to the Northern Ireland Assembly Disqualification Act 1975 (bodies whose members are disqualified) in each case insert at the appropriate places—

"The National Disability Council."

"The Northern Ireland Disability Council."

(8) Consultations which are required by any provision of this Act to be held by the Secretary of State may be held by him before the coming into force of that provision.

SCHEDULES

Section 1(1).

SCHEDULE 1

PROVISIONS SUPPLEMENTING SECTION 1

Impairment

1.—(1) "Mental impairment" includes an impairment resulting from or consisting of a mental illness only if the illness is a clinically well-recognised illness.

(2) Regulations may make provision, for the purposes of this Act—

  (a) for conditions of a prescribed description to be treated as amounting to impairments;

  (b) for conditions of a prescribed description to be treated as not amounting to impairments.

(3) Regulations made under sub-paragraph (2) may make provision as to the meaning of "condition" for the purposes of those regulations.

Long-term effects

2.—(1) The effect of an impairment is a long-term effect if—

  (a) it has lasted at least 12 months;

  (b) the period for which it lasts is likely to be at least 12 months; or

  (c) it is likely to last for the rest of the life of the person affected.

(2) Where an impairment ceases to have a substantial adverse effect on a person's ability to carry out normal day-to-day activities, it is to be treated as continuing to have that effect if that effect is likely to recur.

(3) For the purposes of sub-paragraph (2), the likelihood of an effect recurring shall be disregarded in prescribed circumstances.

(4) Regulations may prescribe circumstances in which, for the purposes of this Act—

  (a) an effect which would not otherwise be a long-term effect is to be treated as such an effect; or

  (b) an effect which would otherwise be a long-term effect is to be treated as not being such an effect.

Severe disfigurement

3.—(1) An impairment which consists of a severe disfigurement is to be treated as having a substantial adverse effect on the ability of the person concerned to carry out normal day-to-day activities.

(2) Regulations may provide that in prescribed circumstances a severe disfigurement is not to be treated as having that effect.

(3) Regulations under sub-paragraph (2) may, in particular, make provision with respect to deliberately acquired disfigurements.

Normal day-to-day activities

4.—(1) An impairment is to be taken to affect the ability of the person concerned to carry out normal day-to-day activities only if it affects one of the following—

  (a) mobility;

  (b) manual dexterity;

  (c) physical co-ordination;

(d) continence;

(e) ability to lift, carry or otherwise move everyday objects;

(f) speech, hearing or eyesight;

(g) memory or ability to concentrate, learn or understand; or

(h) perception of the risk of physical danger.

(2) Regulations may prescribe—

(a) circumstances in which an impairment which does not have an effect falling within sub-paragraph (1) is to be taken to affect the ability of the person concerned to carry out normal day-to-day activities;

(b) circumstances in which an impairment which has an effect falling within sub-paragraph (1) is to be taken not to affect the ability of the person concerned to carry out normal day-to-day activities.

Substantial adverse effects

5. Regulations may make provision for the purposes of this Act—

(a) for an effect of a prescribed kind on the ability of a person to carry out normal day-to-day activities to be treated as a substantial adverse effect;

(b) for an effect of a prescribed kind on the ability of a person to carry out normal day-to-day activities to be treated as not being a substantial adverse effect.

Effect of medical treatment

6.—(1) An impairment which would be likely to have a substantial adverse effect on the ability of the person concerned to carry out normal day-to-day activities, but for the fact that measures are being taken to treat or correct it, is to be treated as having that effect.

(2) In sub-paragraph (1) "measures" includes, in particular, medical treatment and the use of a prosthesis or other aid.

(3) Sub-paragraph (1) does not apply—

(a) in relation to the impairment of a person's sight, to the extent that the impairment is, in his case, correctable by spectacles or contact lenses or in such other ways as may be prescribed; or

(b) in relation to such other impairments as may be prescribed, in such circumstances as may be prescribed.

Persons deemed to be disabled

7.—(1) Sub-paragraph (2) applies to any person whose name is, both on 12th January 1995 and on the date when this paragraph comes into force, in the register of disabled persons maintained under section 6 of the Disabled Persons (Employment) Act 1944.

1944 c. 10.

(2) That person is to be deemed—

(a) during the initial period, to have a disability, and hence to be a disabled person; and

(b) afterwards, to have had a disability and hence to have been a disabled person during that period.

(3) A certificate of registration shall be conclusive evidence, in relation to the person with respect to whom it was issued, of the matters certified.

(4) Unless the contrary is shown, any document purporting to be a certificate of registration shall be taken to be such a certificate and to have been validly issued.

(5) Regulations may provide for prescribed descriptions of person to be deemed to have disabilities, and hence to be disabled persons, for the purposes of this Act.

(6) Regulations may prescribe circumstances in which a person who has been deemed to be a disabled person by the provisions of sub-paragraph (1) or regulations made under sub-paragraph (5) is to be treated as no longer being deemed to be such a person.

(7) In this paragraph—

"certificate of registration" means a certificate issued under regulations made under section 6 of the Act of 1944; and

"initial period" means the period of three years beginning with the date on which this paragraph comes into force.

Progressive conditions

8.—(1) Where—

(a) a person has a progressive condition (such as cancer, multiple sclerosis or muscular dystrophy or infection by the human immunodeficiency virus),

(b) as a result of that condition, he has an impairment which has (or had) an effect on his ability to carry out normal day-to-day activities, but

(c) that effect is not (or was not) a substantial adverse effect,

he shall be taken to have an impairment which has such a substantial adverse effect if the condition is likely to result in his having such an impairment.

(2) Regulations may make provision, for the purposes of this paragraph—

(a) for conditions of a prescribed description to be treated as being progressive;

(b) for conditions of a prescribed description to be treated as not being progressive.

SCHEDULE 2

Past Disabilities

1. The modifications referred to in section 2 are as follows.

2. References in Parts II and III to a disabled person are to be read as references to a person who has had a disability.

3. In section 6(1), after "not disabled" insert "and who have not had a disability".

4. In section 6(6), for "has" substitute "has had".

5. For paragraph 2(1) to (3) of Schedule 1, substitute—

"(1) The effect of an impairment is a long-term effect if it has lasted for at least 12 months.

(2) Where an impairment ceases to have a substantial adverse effect on a person's ability to carry out normal day-to-day activities, it is to be treated as continuing to have that effect if that effect recurs.

(3) For the purposes of sub-paragraph (2), the recurrence of an effect shall be disregarded in prescribed circumstances."

SCHEDULE 3

ENFORCEMENT AND PROCEDURE

PART I

EMPLOYMENT

Conciliation

1.—(1) Where a complaint is presented to an industrial tribunal under section 8 and a copy of it is sent to a conciliation officer, he shall—

(a) if requested to do so by the complainant and respondent, or

(b) if he considers that he has a reasonable prospect of success,

try to promote a settlement of the complaint without its being determined by an industrial tribunal.

(2) Where a person is contemplating presenting such a complaint, a conciliation officer shall, if asked to do so by the potential complainant or potential respondent, try to promote a settlement.

(3) The conciliation officer shall, where appropriate, have regard to the desirability of encouraging the use of other procedures available for the settlement of grievances.

(4) Anything communicated to a conciliation officer in a case in which he is acting under this paragraph shall not be admissible in evidence in any proceedings before an industrial tribunal except with the consent of the person who communicated it.

Restriction on proceedings for breach of Part II

2.—(1) Except as provided by section 8, no civil or criminal proceedings may be brought against any person in respect of an act merely because the act is unlawful under Part II.

(2) Sub-paragraph (1) does not prevent the making of an application for judicial review.

Period within which proceedings must be brought

3.—(1) An industrial tribunal shall not consider a complaint under section 8 unless it is presented before the end of the period of three months beginning when the act complained of was done.

(2) A tribunal may consider any such complaint which is out of time if, in all the circumstances of the case, it considers that it is just and equitable to do so.

(3) For the purposes of sub-paragraph (1)—

(a) where an unlawful act of discrimination is attributable to a term in a contract, that act is to be treated as extending throughout the duration of the contract;

(b) any act extending over a period shall be treated as done at the end of that period; and

(c) a deliberate omission shall be treated as done when the person in question decided upon it.

(4) In the absence of evidence establishing the contrary, a person shall be taken for the purposes of this paragraph to decide upon an omission—

(a) when he does an act inconsistent with doing the omitted act; or

(b) if he has done no such inconsistent act, when the period expires within which he might reasonably have been expected to do the omitted act if it was to be done.

Evidence

4.—(1) In any proceedings under section 8, a certificate signed by or on behalf of a Minister of the Crown and certifying—

(a) that any conditions or requirements specified in the certificate were imposed by a Minister of the Crown and were in operation at a time or throughout a time so specified, or

(b) that an act specified in the certificate was done for the purpose of safeguarding national security,

shall be conclusive evidence of the matters certified.

(2) A document purporting to be such a certificate shall be received in evidence and, unless the contrary is proved, be deemed to be such a certificate.

PART II

DISCRIMINATION IN OTHER AREAS

Restriction on proceedings for breach of Part III

5.—(1) Except as provided by section 25 no civil or criminal proceedings may be brought against any person in respect of an act merely because the act is unlawful under Part III.

(2) Sub-paragraph (1) does not prevent the making of an application for judicial review.

Period within which proceedings must be brought

6.—(1) A county court or a sheriff court shall not consider a claim under section 25 unless proceedings in respect of the claim are instituted before the end of the period of six months beginning when the act complained of was done.

(2) Where, in relation to proceedings or prospective proceedings under section 25, a person appointed in connection with arrangements under section 28 is approached before the end of the period of six months mentioned in sub-paragraph (1), the period allowed by that sub-paragraph shall be extended by two months.

(3) A court may consider any claim under section 25 which is out of time if, in all the circumstances of the case, it considers that it is just and equitable to do so.

(4) For the purposes of sub-paragraph (1)—

(a) where an unlawful act of discrimination is attributable to a term in a contract, that act is to be treated as extending throughout the duration of the contract;

(b) any act extending over a period shall be treated as done at the end of that period; and

(c) a deliberate omission shall be treated as done when the person in question decided upon it.

(5) In the absence of evidence establishing the contrary, a person shall be taken for the purposes of this paragraph to decide upon an omission—

(a) when he does an act inconsistent with doing the omitted act; or

(b) if he has done no such inconsistent act, when the period expires within which he might reasonably have been expected to do the omitted act if it was to be done.

Compensation for injury to feelings

7. In any proceedings under section 25, the amount of any damages awarded as compensation for injury to feelings shall not exceed the prescribed amount.

Evidence

8.—(1) In any proceedings under section 25, a certificate signed by or on behalf of a Minister of the Crown and certifying—

    (a) that any conditions or requirements specified in the certificate were imposed by a Minister of the Crown and were in operation at a time or throughout a time so specified, or

    (b) that an act specified in the certificate was done for the purpose of safeguarding national security,

shall be conclusive evidence of the matters certified.

(2) A document purporting to be such a certificate shall be received in evidence and, unless the contrary is proved, be deemed to be such a certificate.

SCHEDULE 4

Premises Occupied Under Leases

Part I

Occupation by Employer or Trade Organisation

Failure to obtain consent to alteration

1. If any question arises as to whether the occupier has failed to comply with the section 6 or section 15 duty, by failing to make a particular alteration to the premises, any constraint attributable to the fact that he occupies the premises under a lease is to be ignored unless he has applied to the lessor in writing for consent to the making of the alteration.

Joining lessors in proceedings under section 8

2.—(1) In any proceedings under section 8, in a case to which section 16 applies, the complainant or the occupier may ask the tribunal hearing the complaint to direct that the lessor be joined or sisted as a party to the proceedings.

(2) The request shall be granted if it is made before the hearing of the complaint begins.

(3) The tribunal may refuse the request if it is made after the hearing of the complaint begins.

(4) The request may not be granted if it is made after the tribunal has determined the complaint.

(5) Where a lessor has been so joined or sisted as a party to the proceedings, the tribunal may determine—

    (a) whether the lessor has—

        (i) refused consent to the alteration, or

        (ii) consented subject to one or more conditions, and

    (b) if so, whether the refusal or any of the conditions was unreasonable,

(6) If, under sub-paragraph (5), the tribunal determines that the refusal or any of the conditions was unreasonable it may take one or more of the following steps—

    (a) make such declaration as it considers appropriate;

    (b) make an order authorising the occupier to make the alteration specified in the order;

    (c) order the lessor to pay compensation to the complainant.

(7) An order under sub-paragraph (6)(b) may require the occupier to comply with conditions specified in the order.

(8) Any step taken by the tribunal under sub-paragraph (6) may be in substitution for, or in addition to, any step taken by the tribunal under section 8(2).

(9) If the tribunal orders the lessor to pay compensation it may not make an order under section 8(2) ordering the occupier to do so.

Regulations

3. Regulations may make provision as to circumstances in which—

    (a) a lessor is to be taken, for the purposes of section 16 and this Part of this Schedule to have—

        (i) withheld his consent;

        (ii) withheld his consent unreasonably;

        (iii) acted reasonably in withholding his consent;

    (b) a condition subject to which a lessor has given his consent is to be taken to be reasonable;

    (c) a condition subject to which a lessor has given his consent is to be taken to be unreasonable.

Sub-leases etc.

4. The Secretary of State may by regulations make provision supplementing, or modifying, the provision made by section 16 or any provision made by or under this Part of this Schedule in relation to cases where the occupier occupies premises under a sub-lease or sub-tenancy.

Part II

Occupation by Provider of Services

Failure to obtain consent to alteration

5. If any question arises as to whether the occupier has failed to comply with the section 21 duty, by failing to make a particular alteration to premises, any constraint attributable to the fact that he occupies the premises under a lease is to be ignored unless he has applied to the lessor in writing for consent to the making of the alteration.

Reference to court

6.—(1) If the occupier has applied in writing to the lessor for consent to the alteration and—

    (a) that consent has been refused, or

    (b) the lessor has made his consent subject to one or more conditions,

the occupier or a disabled person who has an interest in the proposed alteration to the premises being made, may refer the matter to a county court or, in Scotland, to the sheriff.

(2) In the following provisions of this Schedule "court" includes "sheriff".

(3) On such a reference the court shall determine whether the lessor's refusal was unreasonable or (as the case may be) whether the condition is, or any of the conditions are, unreasonable.

(4) If the court determines—

(a) that the lessor's refusal was unreasonable, or

(b) that the condition is, or any of the conditions are, unreasonable,

it may make such declaration as it considers appropriate or an order authorising the occupier to make the alteration specified in the order.

(5) An order under sub-paragraph (4) may require the occupier to comply with conditions specified in the order.

Joining lessors in proceedings under section 25

7.—(1) In any proceedings on a claim under section 25, in a case to which this Part of this Schedule applies, the plaintiff, the pursuer or the occupier concerned may ask the court to direct that the lessor be joined or sisted as a party to the proceedings.

(2) The request shall be granted if it is made before the hearing of the claim begins.

(3) The court may refuse the request if it is made after the hearing of the claim begins.

(4) The request may not be granted if it is made after the court has determined the claim.

(5) Where a lessor has been so joined or sisted as a party to the proceedings, the court may determine—

(a) whether the lessor has—

(i) refused consent to the alteration, or

(ii) consented subject to one or more conditions, and

(b) if so, whether the refusal or any of the conditions was unreasonable.

(6) If, under sub-paragraph (5), the court determines that the refusal or any of the conditions was unreasonable it may take one or more of the following steps—

(a) make such declaration as it considers appropriate;

(b) make an order authorising the occupier to make the alteration specified in the order;

(c) order the lessor to pay compensation to the complainant.

(7) An order under sub-paragraph (6)(b) may require the occupier to comply with conditions specified in the order.

(8) If the court orders the lessor to pay compensation it may not order the occupier to do so.

Regulations

8. Regulations may make provision as to circumstances in which—

(a) a lessor is to be taken, for the purposes of section 27 and this Part of this Schedule to have—

(i) withheld his consent;

(ii) withheld his consent unreasonably;

(iii) acted reasonably in withholding his consent;

    (b) a condition subject to which a lessor has given his consent is to be taken to be reasonable;

    (c) a condition subject to which a lessor has given his consent is to be taken to be unreasonable.

Sub-leases etc.

9. The Secretary of State may by regulations make provision supplementing, or modifying, the provision made by section 27 or any provision made by or under this Part of this Schedule in relation to cases where the occupier occupies premises under a sub-lease or sub-tenancy.

Section 50(8).

SCHEDULE 5

THE NATIONAL DISABILITY COUNCIL

Status

1.—(1) The Council shall be a body corporate.

(2) The Council is not the servant or agent of the Crown and does not enjoy any status, immunity or privilege of the Crown.

Procedure

2. The Council has power to regulate its own procedure (including power to determine its quorum).

Membership

3.—(1) The Council shall consist of at least 10, but not more than 20, members.

(2) In this Schedule "member", except in sub-paragraph (5)(b), means a member of the Council.

(3) Each member shall be appointed by the Secretary of State.

(4) The Secretary of State shall appoint one member to be chairman of the Council and another member to be its deputy chairman.

(5) The members shall be appointed from among persons who, in the opinion of the Secretary of State—

    (a) have knowledge or experience of the needs of disabled persons or the needs of a particular group, or particular groups, of disabled persons;

    (b) have knowledge or experience of the needs of persons who have had a disability or the needs of a particular group, or particular groups, of such persons; or

    (c) are members of, or otherwise represent, professional bodies or bodies which represent industry or other business interests.

(6) Before appointing any member, the Secretary of State shall consult such persons as he considers appropriate.

(7) In exercising his powers of appointment, the Secretary of State shall try to secure that at all times at least half the membership of the Council consists of disabled persons, persons who have had a disability or the parents or guardians of disabled persons.

Term of office of members

4.—(1) Each member shall be appointed for a term which does not exceed five years but shall otherwise hold and vacate his office in accordance with the terms of his appointment.

(2) A person shall not be prevented from being appointed as a member merely because he has previously been a member.

(3) Any member may at any time resign his office by written notice given to the Secretary of State.

(4) Regulations may make provision for the Secretary of State to remove a member from his office in such circumstances as may be prescribed.

Remuneration

5.—(1) The Secretary of State may pay such remuneration or expenses to any member as he considers appropriate.

(2) The approval of the Treasury is required for any payment made under this paragraph.

Staff

6. The Secretary of State shall provide the Council with such staff as he considers appropriate.

Supplementary regulation-making power

7. The Secretary of State may by regulations make provision—

   (a) as to the provision of information to the Council by the Secretary of State;

   (b) as to the commissioning by the Secretary of State of research to be undertaken on behalf of the Council;

   (c) as to the circumstances in which and conditions subject to which the Council may appoint any person as an adviser;

   (d) as to the payment by the Secretary of State, with the approval of the Treasury, of expenses incurred by the Council.

Annual report

8.—(1) As soon as is practicable after the end of each financial year, the Council shall report to the Secretary of State on its activities during the financial year to which the report relates.

(2) The Secretary of State shall lay a copy of every annual report of the Council before each House of Parliament and shall arrange for such further publication of the report as he considers appropriate.

SCHEDULE 6

CONSEQUENTIAL AMENDMENTS

Employment and Training Act 1973 (c. 50)

1. In section 12(1) of the Employment and Training Act 1973 (duty of Secretary of State to give preference to ex-service men and women in exercising certain powers in respect of disabled persons)—

(a) for "persons registered as handicapped by disablement" substitute "disabled persons"; and

(b) for the words after ""disabled person"" substitute "has the same meaning as in the Disability Discrimination Act 1995."

Employment Protection (Consolidation) Act 1978 (c. 44)

2. In section 136(1) of the Employment Protection (Consolidation) Act 1978 (appeals to Employment Appeal Tribunal), at the end insert—

"(ff) the Disability Discrimination Act 1995."

3. In paragraph 20 of Schedule 13 to that Act (reinstatement or re-engagement of dismissed employees), in sub-paragraph (3)—

(a) in the definition of "relevant complaint of dismissal", omit "or" and at the end insert "or a complaint under section 8 of the Disability Discrimination Act 1995 arising out of a dismissal";

(b) in the definition of "relevant conciliation powers", omit "or" and at the end insert "or paragraph 1 of Schedule 3 to the Disability Discrimination Act 1995"; and

(c) in the definition of "relevant compromise contract" for "or section" substitute "section" and at the end insert "or section 9(2) of the Disability Discrimination Act 1995".

Companies Act 1985 (c. 6)

4. In paragraph 9 of Schedule 7 to the Companies Act 1985 (disclosure in directors' report of company policy in relation to disabled persons), in the definition of "disabled person" in sub-paragraph (4)(b), for "Disabled Persons (Employment) Act 1944" substitute "Disability Discrimination Act 1995".

Local Government and Housing Act 1989 (c. 42)

5. In section 7 of the Local Government and Housing Act 1989 (all staff of a local authority etc. to be appointed on merit), in subsection (2)—

(a) paragraph (a) shall be omitted;

(b) the word "and" at the end of paragraph (d) shall be omitted; and

(c) after paragraph (e) insert—

"; and

(f) sections 5 and 6 of the Disability Discrimination Act 1995 (meaning of discrimination and duty to make adjustments)."

Enterprise and New Towns (Scotland) Act 1990 (c. 35)

6. In section 16 of the Enterprise and New Towns (Scotland) Act 1990 (duty of certain Scottish bodies to give preference to ex-service men and women in exercising powers to select disabled persons for training), in subsection (2), for "said Act of 1944" substitute "Disability Discrimination Act 1995".

SCHEDULE 7
REPEALS

Section 70(5).

Chapter	Short title	Extent of repeal
7 & 8 Geo. 6 c. 10.	The Disabled Persons (Employment) Act 1944.	Section 1. Sections 6 to 14. Section 19. Section 21. Section 22(4).
6 & 7 Eliz. 2 c. 33.	The Disabled Persons (Employment) Act 1958.	Section 2.
1970 c. 44.	The Chronically Sick and Disabled Persons Act 1970.	Section 16.
1978 c. 44.	The Employment Protection (Consolidation) Act 1978.	In Schedule 13, in paragraph 20(3), the word "or" in the definitions of "relevant complaint of dismissal" and "relevant conciliation powers".
1989 c. 42.	The Local Government and Housing Act 1989.	In section 7(2), paragraph (a) and the word "and" at the end of paragraph (d).
1993 c. 62.	The Education Act 1993.	In section 161(5), the words from "and in this subsection" to the end.

SCHEDULE 8

Section 70(6).

MODIFICATIONS OF THIS ACT IN ITS APPLICATION TO NORTHERN IRELAND

1. In its application to Northern Ireland this Act shall have effect subject to the following modifications.

2.—(1) In section 3(1) for "Secretary of State" substitute "Department".

(2) In section 3 for subsections (4) to (12) substitute—

"(4) In preparing a draft of any guidance, the Department shall consult such persons as it considers appropriate.

(5) Where the Department proposes to issue any guidance, the Department shall publish a draft of it, consider any representations that are made to the Department about the draft and, if the Department thinks it appropriate, modify its proposals in the light of any of those representations.

(6) If the Department decides to proceed with any proposed guidance, the Department shall lay a draft of it before the Assembly.

(7) If, within the statutory period, the Assembly resolves not to approve the draft, the Department shall take no further steps in relation to the proposed guidance.

(8) If no such resolution is made within the statutory period, the Department shall issue the guidance in the form of its draft.

(9) The guidance shall come into force on such date as the Department may by order appoint.

(10) Subsection (7) does not prevent a new draft of the proposed guidance being laid before the Assembly.

(11) The Department may—

    (a) from time to time revise the whole or any part of any guidance and re-issue it ;

    (b) by order revoke any guidance.

(12) In this section—

    "the Department" means the Department of Economic Development;

    "guidance" means guidance issued by the Department under this section and includes guidance which has been revised and re-issued;

    "statutory period" has the meaning assigned to it by section 41(2) of the Interpretation Act (Northern Ireland) 1954."

3. In section 4(6) for "Great Britain" substitute "Northern Ireland".

4.—(1) In section 7(2) for "Secretary of State" substitute "Department of Economic Development".

(2) In section 7(4) to (10) for "Secretary of State" wherever it occurs substitute "Department of Economic Development", for "he" and "him" wherever they occur substitute "it" and for "his" wherever it occurs substitute "its".

(3) In section 7(9) for "Parliament" substitute "the Assembly".

5.—(1) In section 8(3) omit "or (in Scotland) in reparation".

(2) In section 8(7) for "paragraph 6A of Schedule 9 to the Employment Protection (Consolidation) Act 1978" substitute "Article 61(3) of the Industrial Relations (Northern Ireland) Order 1976".

6.—(1) In section 9(2)(a) for "a conciliation officer" substitute "the Agency".

(2) In section 9(4) in the definition of "qualified lawyer" for the words from "means" to the end substitute "means a barrister (whether in practice as such or employed to give legal advice) or a solicitor of the Supreme Court who holds a practising certificate.".

7.—(1) In section 10(1)(b) omit "or recognised body".

(2) In section 10(2)(b) for "Secretary of State" substitute "Department of Economic Development".

(3) In section 10(3) in the definition of "charity" for "1993" substitute "(Northern Ireland) 1964", omit the definition of "recognised body" and in the definition of "supported employment" for "Act 1944" substitute "Act (Northern Ireland) 1945".

(4) In section 10(4) for "England and Wales" where it twice occurs substitute "Northern Ireland".

(5) Omit section 10(5).

8.—In section 12(5) for "Great Britain" where it twice occurs substitute "Northern Ireland".

9.—(1) In section 19(3)(g) for "section 2 of the Employment and Training Act 1973" substitute "sections 1 and 2 of the Employment and Training Act (Northern Ireland) 1950".

(2) In section 19(5) for paragraph (a) substitute—

"(a) education which is funded, or secured, by a relevant body or provided at—

(i) an establishment which is funded by such a body or by the Department of Education for Northern Ireland; or

(ii) any other establishment which is a school within the meaning of the Education and Libraries (Northern Ireland) Order 1986;".

(3) For section 19(6) substitute—

"(6) In subsection (5) "relevant body" means—

(a) an education and library board;

(b) a voluntary organisation; or

(c) a body of a prescribed kind.".

10. In section 20(7) for paragraphs (b) and (c) substitute "; or

(b) functions conferred by or under Part VIII of the Mental Health (Northern Ireland) Order 1986 are exercisable in relation to a disabled person's property or affairs.".

11. In section 22(4) and (6) omit "or (in Scotland) the subject of".

12.—(1) In section 25(1) omit "or (in Scotland) in reparation".

(2) In section 25(3) for "England and Wales" substitute "Northern Ireland".

(3) Omit section 25(4).

(4) In section 25(5) omit the words from "or" to the end.

13. In section 26(3) omit "or a sheriff court".

14.—(1) In section 28 for "Secretary of State" wherever it occurs substitute "Department of Health and Social Services".

(2) In section 28(3) and (4) for "he" substitute "it".

(3) In section 28(5) for "Treasury" substitute "Department of Finance and Personnel in Northern Ireland".

15. Omit sections 29, 30 and 31.

16.—(1) In section 32(1) for "Secretary of State" substitute "Department of the Environment".

(2) In section 32(5) for the definition of "taxi" substitute—

""taxi" means a vehicle which—

(a) is licensed under Article 61 of the Road Traffic (Northern Ireland) Order 1981 to stand or ply for hire; and

(b) seats not more than 8 passengers in addition to the driver".

17. In section 33, for "Secretary of State", wherever it occurs, substitute "Department of the Environment".

18. For section 34 substitute—

"New licences conditional on compliance with accessibility taxi regulations.

34.—(1) The Department of the Environment shall not grant a public service vehicle licence under Article 61 of the Road Traffic (Northern Ireland) Order 1981 for a taxi unless the vehicle conforms with those provisions of the taxi accessibility regulations with which it will be required to conform if licensed.

(2) Subsection (1) does not apply if such a licence was in force with respect to the vehicle at any time during the period of 28 days immediately before the day on which the licence is granted.

(3) The Department of the Environment may by order provide for subsection (2) to cease to have effect on such date as may be specified in the order.".

19. Omit section 35.

20. In section 36(7) for "licensing authority" substitute "Department of the Environment".

21.—(1) In section 37(5) and (6) for "licensing authority" substitute "Department of the Environment".

(2) In section 37(9) for "Secretary of State" substitute "Department of the Environment".

22.—(1) In section 38(1) for "a licensing authority" substitute "the Department of the Environment".

(2) In section 38(2) for "licensing authority concerned" substitute "Department of the Environment".

(3) In section 38(3) for the words from "the magistrates' court" to the end substitute "a court of summary jurisdiction acting for the petty sessions district in which the aggrieved person resides".

23. Omit section 39.

24.—(1) In section 40 for "Secretary of State" wherever it occurs substitute "Department of the Environment".

(2) In section 40(5) for the definition of "public service vehicle" substitute—

""public service vehicle" means a vehicle which—

(a) seats more than 8 passengers in addition to the driver; and

(b) is a public service vehicle for the purposes of the Road Traffic (Northern Ireland) Order 1981;".

(3) In section 40(7) for the words from "the Disabled" to the end substitute "such representative organisations as it thinks fit".

25.—(1) In section 41(2) for "Secretary of State" substitute "Department of the Environment".

(2) In section 41 for subsections (3) and (4) substitute—

"(3) Any person who uses a regulated public service vehicle in contravention of this section is guilty of an offence and liable on summary conviction to a fine not exceeding level 4 on the standard scale.".

26.—(1) In section 42 for "Secretary of State" wherever it occurs substitute "Department of the Environment".

(2) In section 42(1) for "he" substitute "it".

(3) In section 42(6) for "his" substitute "its".

27. In section 43 for "Secretary of State" wherever it occurs substitute "Department of the Environment".

28.—(1) In section 44 for "Secretary of State" wherever it occurs substitute "Department of the Environment".

(2) In section 44(2) for "him" substitute "it".

(3) In section 44(6) for "he" substitute "it" and for "his" substitute "its".

29.—(1) In section 45 for "Secretary of State" wherever it occurs substitute "Department of the Environment".

(2) In section 45(2) for "him" substitute "it" and at the end add "of Northern Ireland".

(3) In section 45(4) for "he" substitute "it".

30.—(1) In section 46 for "Secretary of State" wherever it occurs substitute "Department of the Environment".

(2) In section 46(6) in the definition of "rail vehicle" for the words "on any railway, tramway or prescribed system" substitute "by rail".

(3) Omit section 46(7).

(4) In section 46(11) for the words from "the Disabled" to the end substitute "such representative organisations as it thinks fit".

31.—(1) In section 47 for "Secretary of State" wherever it occurs substitute "Department of the Environment".

(2) In section 47(3) for the words "the Disabled Persons Transport Advisory Committee and such other persons as he" substitute "such persons as it" and for "he" substitute "it".

32. Omit section 48(3).

33.—(1) In the heading to Part VI of this Act and in section 50(1) for "National Disability Council" substitute "Northern Ireland Disability Council".

(2) In section 50(2) for "the Secretary of State" in the first place where it occurs substitute "a Northern Ireland department" and in the other place where it occurs substitute "that department".

(3) In section 50(3) for "Secretary of State" substitute "Department of Health and Social Services".

(4) In section 50(7) for "the Secretary of State" substitute "a Northern Ireland department" and after "Crown" insert "or a Northern Ireland department".

(5) In section 50(9)(a) for sub-paragraphs (i) to (iv) substitute—

> "(i) the Disabled Persons (Employment) Act (Northern Ireland) 1945;
>
> (ii) the Contracts of Employment and Redundancy Payments Act (Northern Ireland) 1965;
>
> (iii) the Employment and Training Act (Northern Ireland) 1950;
>
> (iv) the Industrial Relations (Northern Ireland) Orders 1976; or".

(6) In section 50(10) for the words from "time when" to the end substitute "time when—

(a) there are no committees in existence under section 17 of the Disabled Persons (Employment) Act (Northern Ireland) 1945; and

(b) there is no person appointed to act generally under section 60(1) of this Act.".

34.—(1) In section 51(1) for "the Secretary of State" substitute "any Northern Ireland department" and for "the Secretary of State's" substitute "that department's".

(2) In section 51(2) for "The Secretary of State" substitute "A Northern Ireland department".

(3) In section 51(4) for "a county court or a sheriff court" substitute "or a county court".

(4) In section 51(6) for "the Secretary of State" substitute "a Northern Ireland department".

35. For section 52 substitute—

"Further provisions about codes issued under section 51.

52.—(1) In this section—

"proposal" means a proposal made by the Council to a Northern Ireland department under section 51;

"responsible department"—

> (a) in relation to a proposal, means the Northern Ireland department to which the proposal is made,
>
> (b) in relation to a code, means the Northern Ireland department by which the code is issued; and

"statutory period" has the meaning assigned to it by section 41(2) of the Interpretation Act (Northern Ireland) 1954.

(2) In preparing any proposal, the Council shall consult—

> (a) such persons (if any) as the responsible department has specified in making its request to the Council; and
>
> (b) such other persons (if any) as the Council considers appropriate.

(3) Before making any proposal the Council shall publish a draft, consider any representations made to it about the draft and, if it thinks it appropriate, modify its proposal in the light of any of those representations.

(4) Where the Council makes any proposal, the responsible department may—

> (a) approve it;
>
> (b) approve it subject to such modifications as that department thinks appropriate; or
>
> (c) refuse to approve it.

(5) Where the responsible department approves any proposal (with or without modifications) that department shall prepare a draft of the proposed code and lay it before the Assembly.

(6) If, within the statutory period, the Assembly resolves not to approve the draft, the responsible department shall take no further steps in relation to the proposed code.

(7) If no such resolution is made within the statutory period, the responsible department shall issue the code in the form of its draft.

(8) The code shall come into force on such date as the responsible department may appoint by order.

(9) Subsection (6) does not prevent a new draft of the proposed code from being laid before the Assembly.

(10) If the responsible department refuses to approve a proposal, that department shall give the Council a written statement of the department's reasons for not approving it.

(11) The responsible department may by order revoke a code.".

36.—(1) In section 53 for "Secretary of State" wherever it occurs substitute "Department of Economic Development".

(2) In section 53(1) for "he" substitute "it".

(3) In section 53(5) for "a county court or a sheriff court" substitute "or a county court".

37. For section 54 substitute—

"Further provisions about codes issued under section 53.

54.—(1) In preparing a draft of any code under section 53, the Department shall consult such organisations representing the interests of employers or of disabled persons in, or seeking, employment as the Department considers appropriate.

(2) Where the Department proposes to issue a code, the Department shall publish a draft of the code, consider any representations that are made to the Department about the draft and, if the Department thinks it appropriate, modify its proposals in the light of any of those representations.

(3) If the Department decides to proceed with the code, the Department shall lay a draft of it before the Assembly.

(4) If, within the statutory period, the Assembly resolves not to approve the draft, the Department shall take no further steps in relation to the proposed code.

(5) If no such resolution is made within the statutory period, the Department shall issue the code in the form of its draft.

(6) The code shall come into force on such date as the Department may appoint by order.

(7) Subsection (4) does not prevent a new draft of the proposed code from being laid before the Assembly.

(8) The Department may by order revoke a code.

(9) In this section—

"the Department" means the Department of Economic Development; and

"statutory period" has the meaning assigned to it by section 41(2) of the Interpretation Act (Northern Ireland) 1954.".

38. In section 56(2) and (4) for "Secretary of State" substitute "Department of Economic Development".

39. In section 59(1) after "Crown" where it twice occurs insert "or a Northern Ireland department".

40.—(1) In section 60(1) to (3) for "Secretary of State" wherever it occurs substitute "Department of Economic Development" and for "he" and "him" wherever they occur substitute "it".

(2) In section 60(4) for "Treasury" substitute "Department of Finance and Personnel in Northern Ireland".

SCH. 8

(3) For section 60(6) substitute—

"(6) The Department of Economic Development may by order repeal section 17 of, and Schedule 2 to, the Disabled Persons (Employment) Act (Northern Ireland) 1945 (district advisory committees).".

(4) In section 60(7) omit "paragraph (b) of", for "1944" substitute "1945" and omit "in each case".

(5) In section 60, omit subsection (8).

41. For section 61 substitute—

"Amendments of Disabled Persons (Employment) Act (Northern Ireland) 1945.

61.—(1) Section 15 of the Disabled Persons (Employment) Act (Northern Ireland) 1945 (which gives the Department of Economic Development power to make arrangements for the provision of supported employment) is amended as set out in subsections (2) to (5).

(2) In subsection (1)—

(a) for "persons registered as handicapped by disablement" substitute "disabled persons";

(b) for "their disablement" substitute "their disability"; and

(c) for "are not subject to disablement" substitute "do not have a disability".

(3) In subsection (2) for the words from "any of one or more companies" to "so required and prohibited" substitute "any company, association or body".

(4) After subsection (2) insert—

"(2A) The only kind of company which the Department itself may form in exercising its powers under this section is a company which is—

(a) required by its constitution to apply its profits, if any, or other income in promoting its objects; and

(b) prohibited by its constitution from paying any dividend to its members.".

(5) After subsection (5) insert—

"(5A) For the purposes of this section—

(a) a person is a disabled person if he is a disabled person for the purposes of the Disability Discrimination Act 1995; and

(b) "disability" has the same meaning as in that Act.".

(6) The provisions of section 16 of the Act of 1945 (preference to be given under section 15 of that Act to ex-service men and women) shall become subsection (1) of that section and at the end insert—

"and whose disability is due to that service.

(2) For the purposes of subsection (1) of this section, a disabled person's disability shall be treated as due to service of a particular kind only in such circumstances as may be prescribed."

(7) The following provisions of the Act of 1945 shall cease to have effect—

(a) section 1 (definition of "disabled person");

(b) sections 2 to 4 (training for disabled persons);

(c) sections 6 to 8 (the register of disabled persons);

(d) sections 9 to 11 (obligations on employers with substantial staffs to employ quota of registered persons);

(e) section 12 (the designated employment scheme for persons registered as handicapped by disablement);

(f) section 13 (interpretation of provisions repealed by this Act);

(g) section 14 (records to be kept by employer);

(h) section 19 (proceedings in relation to offences);

(j) sections 21 and 22 (supplementary).

(8) Any statutory provision in which "disabled person" is defined by reference to the Act of 1945 shall be construed as if that expression had the same meaning as in this Act.".

42.—(1) In section 62(2) for "Secretary of State" substitute "Department of Economic Development".

(2) In section 62(7) for "Great Britain" where it twice occurs substitute "Northern Ireland".

43. Omit section 63.

44.—(1) In section 64(3) for "England and Wales" substitute "Northern Ireland".

(2) Omit section 64(4).

(3) In section 64(5)(a) omit the words from ", the British" to the end.

(4) In section 64(8)—

(a) omit the definitions of "British Transport Police", "Royal Parks Constabulary" and "United Kingdom Atomic Energy Authority Constabulary";

(b) in the definition of "the 1947 Act" at the end add "as it applies both in relation to the Crown in right of Her Majesty's Government in Northern Ireland and in relation to the Crown in right of Her Majesty's Government in the United Kingdom";

(c) in the definition of "fire brigade" for the words from "means" to the end substitute "has the same meaning as in the Fire Services (Northern Ireland) Order 1984";

(d) in the definition of "prison officer" for the words from "means" to the end substitute "means any individual who holds any post, otherwise than as a medical officer, to which he has been appointed under section 2(2) of the Prison Act (Northern Ireland) 1953 or who is a prison custody officer within the meaning of Chapter III of Part VIII of the Criminal Justice and Public Order Act 1994";

(e) in the definition of "service for purposes of a Minister of the Crown or government department" at the end add "or service as the head of a Northern Ireland department".

45. Omit section 65.

46. For section 67 substitute—

"Regulations and orders etc.   67.—(1) Any power under this Act to make regulations or orders shall be exercisable by statutory rule for the purposes of the Statutory Rules (Northern Ireland) Order 1979.

(2) Any such power may be exercised to make different provision for different cases, including different provision for different areas or localities.

(3) Any such power, includes power—

(a) to make such incidental, supplementary, consequential or transitional provision as appears to the Northern Ireland department exercising the power to be expedient; and

(b) to provide for a person to exercise a discretion in dealing with any matter.

(4) No order shall be made under section 50(3) unless a draft of the order has been laid before and approved by a resolution of the Assembly.

(5) Any other order made under this Act, other than an order under section 3(9), 52(8), 54(6) or 70(3), and any regulations made under this Act shall be subject to negative resolution within the meaning of section 41(6) of the Interpretation Act (Northern Ireland) 1954 as if they were statutory instruments within the meaning of that Act.

(6) Section 41(3) of the Interpretation Act (Northern Ireland) 1954 shall apply in relation to any instrument or document which by virtue of this Act is required to be laid before the Assembly as if it were a statutory instrument or statutory document within the meaning of that Act.

(7) Subsection (1) does not require an order under section 43 which applies only to a specified vehicle, or to vehicles of a specified person, to be made by statutory rule.

(8) Nothing in section 40(6) or 46(5) affects the powers conferred by subsections (2) and (3)."

47.—(1) For section 68(1) substitute—

"(1) In this Act—

"accessibility certificate" means a certificate issued under section 41(1)(a);

"act" includes a deliberate omission;

"the Agency" means the Labour Relations Agency;

"approval certificate" means a certificate issued under section 42(4);

"the Assembly" means the Northern Ireland Assembly;

"benefits", in Part II, has the meaning given in section 4(4);

"the Department of Economic Development" means the Department of Economic Development in Northern Ireland;

"the Department of the Environment" means the Department of the Environment for Northern Ireland;

"the Department of Health and Social Services" means the Department of Health and Social Services for Northern Ireland;

"employment" means, subject to any prescribed provision, employment under a contract of service or of apprenticeship or a contract personally to do work and related expressions are to be construed accordingly;

"employment at an establishment in Northern Ireland" is to be construed in accordance with subsections (2) to (5);

"enactment" means any statutory provision within the meaning of section 1(f) of the Interpretation Act (Northern Ireland) 1954;

"government department" means a Northern Ireland department or a department of the Government of the United Kingdom;

"Minister of the Crown" includes the Treasury;

"Northern Ireland department" includes (except in sections 51 and 52) the head of a Northern Ireland department;

"occupational pension scheme" has the same meaning as in the Pension Schemes (Northern Ireland) Act 1993;

"premises", includes land of any description;

"prescribed" means prescribed by regulations;

"profession" includes any vocation or occupation;

"provider of services" has the meaning given in section 19(2)(b);

"public service vehicle" and "regulated public service vehicle" have the meaning given in section 40;

"PSV accessibility regulations" means regulations made under section 40(1);

"rail vehicle" and "regulated rail vehicle" have the meaning given in section 46;

"rail vehicle accessibility regulations" means regulations made under section 46(1);

"regulations" means—

    (a) in Parts I and II of this Act, section 66, the definition of "employment" above and subsections (3) and (4) below, regulations made by the Department of Economic Development;

    (b) in Part V of this Act, regulations made by the Department of the Environment;

    (c) in any other provision of this Act, regulations made by the Department of Health and Social Services.

"section 6 duty" means any duty imposed by or under section 6;

"section 15 duty" means any duty imposed by or under section 15;

"section 21 duty" means any duty imposed by or under section 21;

"taxi" and "regulated taxi" have the meaning given in section 32;

"taxi accessibility regulations" means regulations made under section 32(1);

"trade" includes any business;

"trade organisation" has the meaning given in section 13;

"vehicle examiner" means an officer of the Department of the Environment authorised by that Department for the purposes of sections 41 and 42.".

(2) In section 68(2) to (4) for "Great Britain" wherever it occurs substitute "Northern Ireland".

48.—(1) In section 70(3) for "Secretary of State" substitute "Department of Health and Social Services".

(2) In section 70(8) for "the Secretary of State" substitute "a Northern Ireland department" and for "him" substitute "it".

49.—(1) In Schedule 1 in paragraph 7(1) for "Act 1944" substitute "Act (Northern Ireland) 1945".

(2) In Schedule 1 in paragraph 7(7) for "1944" substitute "1945".

50.—(1) In Schedule 3 in paragraph 1—

  (a) for "a conciliation officer" wherever it occurs substitute "the Agency";

(b) in sub-paragraphs (1) and (4) for "he" substitute "it";

(c) in sub-paragraph (3) for "the conciliation officer" substitute "the Agency".

(2) In Schedule 3 for paragraph 4(1) substitute—

"(1) In any proceedings under section 8—

(a) a certificate signed by or on behalf of a Minister of the Crown or a Northern Ireland department and certifying that any conditions or requirements specified in the certificate were imposed by that Minister or that department (as the case may be) and were in operation at a time or throughout a time so specified; or

(b) a certificate signed by or on behalf of the Secretary of State and certifying that an act specified in the certificate was done for the purpose of safeguarding national security,

shall be conclusive evidence of the matters certified.".

(3) In Schedule 3 in paragraph 6(1) omit "or a sheriff court".

(4) In Schedule 3 for paragraph 8(1) substitute—

"(1) In any proceedings under section 25—

(a) a certificate signed by or on behalf of a Minister of the Crown or a Northern Ireland department and certifying that any conditions or requirements specified in the certificate were imposed by that Minister or that department (as the case may be) and were in operation at a time or throughout a time so specified; or

(b) a certificate signed by or on behalf of the Secretary of State and certifying that an act specified in the certificate was done for the purpose of safeguarding national security,

shall be conclusive evidence of the matters certified.".

51.—(1) In Schedule 4 in paragraphs 2(1) and (5) and 7(1) and (5) omit "or sisted".

(2) In Schedule 4 in paragraph 4 for "Secretary of State" substitute "Department of Economic Development".

(3) In Schedule 4 in paragraph 6(1) omit "or, in Scotland, to the sheriff".

(4) In Schedule 4 omit paragraph 6(2).

(5) In Schedule 4 in paragraph 9 for "Secretary of State" substitute "Department of Health and Social Services".

52.—(1) In Schedule 5 in the heading for "National" substitute "Northern Ireland".

(2) In Schedule 5 for "Secretary of State" wherever it occurs substitute "Department of Health and Social Services".

(3) In Schedule 5 in paragraphs 3(6), 5(1), 6 and 8(2) for "he" substitute "it" and in paragraph 3(7) for "his" substitute "its".

(4) In Schedule 5 in paragraphs 5(2) and 7(d) for "Treasury" substitute "Department of Finance and Personnel in Northern Ireland".

(5) In Schedule 5 in paragraph 8(2) for "each House of Parliament" substitute "the Assembly".

53. For Schedules 6 and 7 substitute—

"SCHEDULE 6

CONSEQUENTIAL AMENDMENTS

The Industrial Relations (Northern Ireland) Order 1976 (NI 16)

1. In Article 68(6) of the Industrial Relations (Northern Ireland) Order 1976 (reinstatement or re-engagement of dismissed employees)—

   (a) in the definition of "relevant complaint of dismissal", omit "or" and at the end insert "or a complaint under section 8 of the Disability Discrimination Act 1995 arising out of a dismissal";

   (b) in the definition of "relevant conciliation powers", omit "or" and at the end insert "or paragraph 1 of Schedule 3 to the Disability Discrimination Act 1995";

   (c) in the definition of "relevant compromise contract" for "or Article" substitute "Article" and at the end insert "or section 9(2) of the Disability Discrimination Act 1995".

The Companies (Northern Ireland) Order 1986 (NI 6)

3. In paragraph 9 of Schedule 7 to the Companies (Northern Ireland) Order 1986 (disclosure in directors' report of company policy in relation to disabled persons) in the definition of "disabled person" in sub-paragraph (4)(b) for "Disabled Persons (Employment) Act (Northern Ireland) 1945" substitute "Disability Discrimination Act 1995".

SCHEDULE 7

REPEALS

Chapter	Short title	Extent of repeal
1945 c. 6 (N.I.)	The Disabled Persons (Employment) Act (Northern Ireland) 1945.	Sections 1 to 4. Sections 6 to 14. In section 16 the words "vocational training and industrial rehabilitation courses and", the words "courses and" and the words from "and in selecting" to "engagement". Section 19. Section 21. Section 22.
1960 c. 4 (N.I.)	The Disabled Persons (Employment) Act (Northern Ireland) 1960.	The whole Act.

SCH. 8

Chapter	Short title	Extent of repeal
1976 NI16	The Industrial Relations (Northern Ireland) Order 1976.	In Article 68(6) the word "or" in the definitions of "relevant complaint of dismissal" and "relevant conciliation powers".".

Printed in the UK by The Stationery Office Limited
under the authority and superintendence of Carol Tullo, Controller of
Her Majesty's Stationery Office and Queen's Printer of Acts of Parliament

1st Impression November 1995
5th Impression August 1999
8/99   19585   Job No.0090729